RAOUL MOAT
HIS SHORT LIFE AND BLOODY DEATH

RAOUL MOAT
HIS SHORT LIFE AND BLOODY DEATH

VANESSA HOWARD

JOHN BLAKE

Published by John Blake Publishing Ltd,
3 Bramber Court, 2 Bramber Road,
London W14 9PB, England

www.blake.co.uk

First published in paperback in 2010

ISBN 978-1-84358-324-0

All rights reserved. No part of this publication may be reproduced,
stored in a retrieval system, or in any form or by any means, without
the prior permission in writing of the publisher, nor be otherwise circulated
in any form of binding or cover other than that in which it is published
and without a similar condition including this condition being imposed
on the subsequent publisher.

British Library Cataloguing-in-Publication Data:

A catalogue record for this book is available from the British Library.

Design by www.envydesign.co.uk

Printed in Great Britain by CPI Bookmarque, Croydon, CR0 4TD

1 3 5 7 9 10 8 6 4 2

© Text copyright Vanessa Howard 2010

All images courtesy of the Press Association.

Papers used by John Blake Publishing are natural, recyclable products
made from wood grown in sustainable forests. The manufacturing processes
conform to the environmental regulations of the country of origin.

Every attempt has been made to contact the relevant copyright-holders,
but some were unobtainable. We would be grateful if the
appropriate people could contact us.

CONTENTS

PROLOGUE	VII
CHAPTER ONE	1
CHAPTER TWO	19
CHAPTER THREE	31
CHAPTER FOUR	47
CHAPTER FIVE	61
CHAPTER SIX	77
CHAPTER SEVEN	91
CHAPTER EIGHT	107
CHAPTER NINE	127
CHAPTER TEN	141
CHAPTER ELEVEN	151

CHAPTER TWELVE	165
CHAPTER THIRTEEN	173
CHAPTER FOURTEEN	185
CHAPTER FIFTEEN	197
CHAPTER SIXTEEN	227
CHAPTER SEVENTEEN	235
CHAPTER EIGHTEEN	261
CHAPTER NINETEEN	267

PROLOGUE

Watch and see what happens
– from Raoul Moat's Facebook page

When the end came, it seemed inevitable. How else could it end?

The figure was picked out in green using night-vision technology; he was lying on soaking wet grass as police dogs barked and officers shouted out into the darkness. The tension between those on the ground had been stretched out over six hours. Perhaps Britain's most wanted man knew that this was the moment; one firm squeeze of the trigger and it would be all over.

Even amongst those who hadn't followed the 24-hour news coverage, few would be surprised to wake on the morning of Saturday 10 July to hear that Raoul Moat had been shot and killed. He had been cornered on the side of the river bank in the now infamous town of Rothbury since seven o'clock on Friday evening. He had finally been surrounded by snipers as part of the police operation, the scale of which was almost unprecedented.

In the days leading up to these final moments, the public had learned more details about the resources that had been used to find Moat. Hundreds of officers from 15 police forces had been recruited for the hunt, specialist advice had been sought from the British Army, the Police National Search Centre, and even the heat-seeking technology of a £20m RAF Tornado jet had been employed. The final cost of the operation would mount to more than three million pounds. All to track one man.

There were those who thought the use of so much firepower was risible, news that armoured vehicles from Northern Ireland had arrived to patrol the quiet streets of Rothbury was remarked on as excessive. Yet when Moat went on the run, it was only four weeks after Derrick Bird had shot dead 12 people and injured 11 more in and around the quiet country lanes of Cumbria. How else could Northumbria Police have been expected to respond?

A madman was on the loose, a self-declared maniac; a man who had killed one man, seriously injured his former partner, and shot a police officer in the face. He had declared war on the police and, as the days of his week-long evasion unfolded, he threatened to shoot members of the public. *The rules had changed* he had warned in a taped message left for the police to find. The hunted had become the hunter. The authorities were under no illusion as to what Moat was capable of and he had made his intentions clear in a letter that he had handed to a friend in which he had stated: *I won't stop till I'm dead*.

How had it come to this? What had driven one man to cause such terrible suffering to the families of his victims? Had he suffered a catastrophic breakdown or had the signs of his collapse been evident for years to all who had encountered him? What had turned a loving father into a monster, a man who would declare war on the police?

Perhaps this was no more than a freak event, something so rare as to offer little insight into what can destabilise an ordinary man.

Yet the truth, even as it emerges in a fractured and partial way, suggests something that has far-reaching and even terrifying implications. All the signs were there: this was a man who had already brought misery to the lives of others, a person who had known years of destructive rages and yet was also someone who had asked for help.

He knew that he suffered from what he described as 'areas of fault', dark parts of his psyche that he feared: rages that surfaced in him and that he could not control.

The youngster in the baby pictures, the plump-faced and bright-eyed boy, would would become a killer, a man his mother would no longer recognise. Step by step, he walked a path of destruction and no one helped him find another way. He wanted help. None came, or at least, if and when it did it was too little and too late. Now he would ensure that everyone would pay, that the whole world would learn his name and there was only one way it would end.

We know the name yet do we know other Raoul Moats? Other men in other communities waiting for the killer inside them to emerge and take control. For Moat is no one-off, his was not a isolated act of revenge. Other people whose thinking mirrors his are out there.

This book will reveal how disturbed minds such as Moat's are formed and how, as a society, we need to understand why Moat is now an antihero to many. There is a dark undercurrent of disaffection that, should it settle in the mind of someone battling instability and grievances, can yield terrifying results.

CHAPTER ONE
FREEDOM
THURSDAY 1 JULY

Most of what I've done I've gotten away with, no arrest.
— from Raoul Moat's letters

Those who've been incarcerated behind HM Prison Durham's bleak and imposing walls may well be amused to learn that its architect was imprisoned as it was being built for theft of the funds intended for its construction.

Perhaps it was not an auspicious start for a building that has housed some of Britain's most infamous 'hard men' criminals over the last two hundred years, names like John McVicar, Frankie Fraser, Ronnie and Reggie Kray. As well as men with a reputation for violence, Durham has housed female serial killers such as the arsenic poisoner Mary Ann

Cotton. It is believed that she was responsible for the deaths of 21 victims and she was hanged at the gaol in 1873. More recently, the prison inmates have included Rose West and Myra Hindley.

Yet its notorious reputation perhaps belies the fact that it is no longer a Category A prison but a Category B. Once it held the country's most violent and highly dangerous inmates but, with its downgrade, it now acts as a local prison for convicted and remand adult male prisoners, primarily serving the courts of County Durham, Tyne and Wear and Teesside. Men who the authorities decide do not require maximum security and who often serve short-term sentences. Men like Raoul Thomas Moat.

Despite its harsh appearance, HM Prison Durham has been undergoing a substantial re-fit over the last ten years and is perhaps better equipped than ever to deal with its migrating population. When the prison hit the headlines seven years ago because figures were released showing it had the highest suicide rate of any English gaol, refurbishment may well have been overdue. Coping with the often complex social and psychological needs of prisoners is far from straightforward. Many have known years of alcohol or drug abuse or both, and many more grew up in dysfunctional households or spent periods of time in care. A lack of consistent and nurturing parental attention leaves many young men ill-prepared to deal with stress, often meaning that they resort to violence when needs are not met or if a threat, real or imagined, is identified.

On top of these psychological problems, some of the prisoner population also face practical difficulties. It is thought that anywhere between a third to two-thirds of prisoners are functionally illiterate and the effect of the failure to rehabilitate prisoners has led the Howard League for Penal Reform to report that two-thirds can be expected to re-offend within two years.

Prison, then, can be a fraught environment. Whilst there are those who take responsibility for their actions and see a custodial sentence as an opportunity to change their behaviour, they remain in the minority. Help is on hand: literacy tuition, courses in woodwork, bricklaying, painting and decorating and even, with a nod to the twenty-first century, Data Inputting. Giving a structure and direction to inmates' time is important but with shorter sentences, there is no simple route to rehabilitation. There is no magic wand.

A man like Raoul Moat will not have cut a remarkable figure walking the halls and walkways of Durham. True, he was tall and physically imposing at 6ft 3in and had the physique of someone who was committed to body building; yet even impressive physical attributes are not uncommon amongst those who are convicted. The gym is perhaps the busiest section of any prison and body building is a common obsession for men inside. It is easy to guess its attractions: whilst gaining bulk, men radiate the signal that they are not to be messed with, and even those who are incarcerated for the first time will seek to present an image of themselves as untouchable once behind bars. Besides, boredom is the main and overriding factor in any jail term. It is not unheard of for prisoners to spend 18 hours locked in their cells and 'working out' is a simple distraction.

With his bulk and all the swagger he'd mustered as a former nightclub doorman, Moat was determined that from the moment he arrived to serve his first custodial sentence, he would not be cowed or intimidated. And, sure enough, he found his way and soon he was vocal about just what he was capable of. No one would mess with Raoul Moat.

It was not as if he would be a familiar face in his Housing Block for long. He was there to serve a sentence for assault but would be held for only two months and two days. Not long enough to really make his presence felt and with insufficient time to be dealt with by the Probation Service. Those who serve a sentence of less than 12 months are released with no requirements for them to comply with in the community, such as attending drug rehabilitation.

If that seems surprising, it is worth noting that well over 100,000 prisoners were released last year alone, making the task of assessment and evaluation of risk and ongoing supervision an impossible task without a huge commitment towards raising staffing numbers, and improving training and resources.

As things stand, it is a fact that many ex-prisoners will not be supervised and it is inevitable that some will fall though the cracks as they re-enter civilian life. Men like Moat, with a long and growing list of arrests and convictions over a period of years, characters who repeatedly offend and pose a particular risk to society but not always in ways that can be foreseen.

A lot of research and work has been carried out over recent years into offending and rehabilitation and it has had an impact not only on the prison and probation service but on police behaviour too. Intelligence-led policing is one example. It was developed in response to the fact that a high percentage of crimes are carried out by a proportionately small number of offenders.

The thinking is that if those repeat-offenders can be identified, targeted and dealt with, a significant number of incidents should be prevented. Northumbria Police led the way by targeting shoplifters, some of whom had over 100 arrests to their names: a small group capable of causing retailers to lose thousands of pounds each year. Northumbria's intelligence-led policing initiative saw shoplifting offences fall by a third.

But Moat was no shoplifter, a crime he would have thought beneath him. Moat saw himself as a gentleman, a man with an outward persona of calm and control but he also knew how to display his 'bad boy' credentials, to leave no one in doubt that he was a guy who knew how to navigate his way around Newcastle's criminal underbelly. He was someone who was capable of administering a beating if he felt that he had been disrespected and, what was more, he was someone who was used to giving the police the run-around.

He'd been arrested before but it had come to nothing, and besides, he boasted that he'd got away with a lot more, any number of crimes that had never been detected. Now that he was banged up it was inconvenient, nothing more. But the truth was a lot more disconcerting than the tough-guy image he portrayed. He was not inside for armed robbery or for fighting with police officers; he was in prison for assaulting a minor, a child. Moat reportedly had 6 children with various different women and his violent disposition led to domestic assault.

A string of arrests stretching back 10 years and charges for carrying weaponry would be easy to dismiss and even be something to boast of. But a man serving time for hurting a child is at risk once within prison. A code, such as it is, leaves anyone with convictions for sexual offences open targets for other prisoners' aggression once in jail, and it is commonplace to hear of abusers being hit, cut or scalded by fellow inmates and frequently they are segregated from other prisoners.

The greater their notoriety, the more likely they are to

be targeted. Ian Huntley, for example, was hospitalised in March 2010 after another inmate was said to have slashed his throat; this was merely the latest in a number of physical attacks since his conviction of the murders of Holly Wells and Jessica Chapman.

There is an unspoken hierarchy in prisons, with respect determined by the nature of the crime committed, time served and contacts in the outside criminal world. Moat felt he could not be seen as someone who hurt children. This perception of him could have had serious and ongoing repercussions during the time he was locked up, no matter how brief this might be. Moat was many things but he was not a stupid man. He knew how important preconceived ideas were and was aware that he would have to make it clear that he was banged up for something he had not done.

He didn't hit the kid, he asserted. Don't get him wrong: giving a kid a clip round the ear was perfectly acceptable to his mind if the child was out of order, they needed to be taught when they'd stepped out of line. But this wasn't what had happened this time, he didn't hit his kids, and he wasn't going to take the easier route of pleading guilty in order to get away with a community service order or the like. He took a stand, saying he wasn't guilty, and when the judge told him that he'd be serving time, he'd looked over towards the bench and said that they were sending down an innocent man.

Moat believed that the police and social workers interfere and only see that they want to see. To many prisoners he was pushing on an open door when he spoke of his suspicion that the police were on his case and happy to fit people up when it suited them. He maintained that officers had a vendetta against him and that they always had, pulling him over time and time again for no reason. Not only were they idiots, they were out to bully either those that had done nothing of consequence, old women who hadn't paid their TV licences, or they would latch on to someone like him, someone who knew how to stand up to them, and they would persecute him, orchestrating a witch-hunt. He hated the police and thought that they should be careful not to push him too far.

There were more than a few who agreed with Moat. He articulated a wider belief that the police didn't serve their communities and that administering law and order was actually done by men like Moat, who settled disputes and made clear the rights and wrongs of a situation. Moat was verbally adept but, while he was surrounded by men who found themselves in agreement with him, in his own mind, he could not shake free his fears about the true nature of his predicament.

He was a 37-year-old man with a string of broken relationships behind him, a brother and mother he had not seen for years, with daughters by different mothers who had been taken from him, his business had failed, and he needed medication to try and suppress his intermittent fits of panic and depression. He was also single again. Sam, his girlfriend of six years, the mother of his youngest daughter, had told him their relationship was over. She changed her status on her Facebook to 'single'. She wanted no more to do with him. He was a loser.

She had visited him inside only once. Moat was always proud of the way Sam looked, she was young, 15 years younger than him, and she was petite and pretty, just the sort of girl he imagined should be on his arm and waiting in the visiting centre to see him. The problem was that she was there to talk about their daughter Chanel and to tell him that, for her sake, he should not have contact with his youngest daughter once he was released. As a couple they had a stormy relationship. Moat knew he had a temper and that he could lose his cool. He started yelling at Sam and stood up, his aggression evident to everyone in the visiting room. Prison staff had to intervene and Sam left.

He could not get Sam and his daughter out of his mind. How could Sam have done this to him? After all he had done, she knew that he was in prison because he was making a stand against being falsely accused. He'd have to call her and sort things out. Two days before his release, he managed to track her down and talk to her on her mobile. She was blunt and told him that it was over between them and what was more, for the first time she had found someone that she really liked. Sam asked him to please respect her decision to move on and to leave her alone.

The call had taken but two minutes but the impact on Moat was immediate. He cracked, telling anyone who would listen to him that he had lost everything. To other inmates and the prison officers who had observed him talking on the phone, this was a departure from the persona he had presented since he first walked into Durham. He had lost weight whilst inside; perhaps with limited access to the gym and protein shakes that maintained mass this was to be expected, but possibly something else was plaguing him. That night, Moat couldn't sleep and he began to tell all who would listen that everything that had mattered to him had been taken away.

Amongst fellow prisoners, Moat would have seen a surge of sympathy. Once in prison, the sense of powerlessness is hard to avoid. You are told when to wake, when to sleep, when to eat and when to wash. This is a regime, even if it is a benign one, and you have little control over the pattern of your day. Inside your head is a different matter but it is hard to mentally block off the external realities of life behind bars.

Prison is not about physical punishment, and it has long ago stopped being about hard labour. The hard labour now takes place in the mind. All regular freedoms have been lost and for certain men, the changing nature of relationships of loved ones on the outside can be an additional difficulty.

For some, losing a grip on the lives of those who have defined them, for example losing their status as husband and father, is a far more punishing experience than months lost behind bars.

To prison staff, it was clear that Moat was not coping well with his partner's decision to leave the relationship. He was a man who had been prescribed antidepressants and he was to be released only two days after he heard that Samantha no longer wanted to see him. Raoul Moat began telling people that he had nothing to live for, but this was more than despair. The disturbed man had another piece of information that made him very, very angry. Samantha had a new boyfriend and he was a police officer. She had dumped him and taken up with a copper.

To Samantha, this was the clearest way to send a signal to her ex that she was not to be approached. With his arrests, the convictions and now a spell in prison, Moat would clearly realise that, in the eyes of the law, he was walking on thin ice. To start messing around or trying to intimidate a police officer's girlfriend would be very risky, he'd obviously realise that. As stated previously, Moat wasn't a stupid man, he would understand that she was now beyond his reach and that his threats would do more than just upset her, they could mean that the full force of the law would be brought to bear against him. Why would he risk that?

Samantha's hope was to make Moat accept that their

relationship was over. He did accept this, but with acceptance came a terrifying rage and the impulse to unleash his anger against those who had crossed him.

In some respects, this was nothing new in his character. He'd spoken on several occasions of men he'd beaten, those who'd let him down, such as the story of the young man he'd helped out once but who, in the end, he had thrashed for one indiscretion or another. There was a dividing line in Moat's head. He could play the perfect gentleman, the quiet and solicitous soul, but should that line be crossed, there would be hell to pay.

As he ranted that Sam had betrayed him, prison staff saw the warning signs. Men with Moat's profile don't tend to process disappointment in any rational or measured way. Instead and all too often, they lash out.

After a day and night without sleep Moat looked exhausted, but something more sinister was afoot. He was thinking, thinking hard and planning. If he could get to Sam, talk to her, perhaps she'd come round – she had in the past when they'd had their rocky moments. This was about more than the two of them, she had to see that – there was their daughter to think about. He asked to speak with the prison's priest, he talked of suicidal feelings, and it seemed that his rage when not aimed at others turned inwards, and made him question whether he wanted to live or die.

Raoul Moat knew how difficult life could be once a relationship with the mother of his children broke down.

His other daughters had eventually come to live with him, but not before a bitter battle with his ex. And that had meant interference, social workers snooping around and asking questions. One of his lowest moments came when he realised that this time, he was facing a custodial sentence. That meant losing his daughters once again. Now, with a record that showed that he'd done time, where did he stand in the eyes of the authorities? Now he'd be painted as an unfit father with a history of violence and law breaking. Without the children to care for, he'd lose his council home too. Moat now felt that he had to draw a line, he had to take control.

By the day of his release, a Thursday, there was a lot on his mind. He was 48 hours into examining the implications of his situation and assessing his options. A lot of his focus was on Sam. She wanted their partnership to be over but Moat could not accept this. It would never be over, he reasoned.

He shook hands with the men he'd come to know behind bars, one or two were already familiar to him from life on the outside anyway, guys he'd come across during his time as a doorman. They all felt for him, he could sense that much. Each of them dreaded facing up to what a prison term could do to closest family members, to anyone's chances of employment, and were aware of how a record could cast a long shadow over any plans for the future. There were commiserations all round.

As he'd served a sentence of less than 12 months, he would be processed like any other man over the age of 21 who'd completed a short sentence. Release meant being freed without restriction, he would not be out on licence with conditions attached, requiring him to attend drug or alcohol rehabilitation. Nor would he be required to inform the authorities as to where he'd be living or to stay away from his previous partner or victim. He was free. Free to act.

The staff within Durham had observed Moat and although he would not be assigned a probation worker, there were steps they could take to alert the police should they have any concerns about the possibility of a released prisoner's state of mind or declared intentions. A Security Information Report is normally compiled and forwarded to the police.

These reports are viewed as an essential tool for managing offenders. In fact, in February 2010 all prison governors were informed that they are a key part of the strategy for dealing with PPOs (Prolific and other Priority Offenders). The report, from the Ministry of Justice's National Offender Management Service, describes its purpose as follows:

…to concentrate resources on the small proportion of offenders whose volume of offending has caused significant impact in their local community. This cohort of offenders can have a variety of contact with the criminal justice system, including offenders under

no statutory supervision, those serving community sentences and those serving custodial sentences, including those serving less than 12 months.

Clearly, Moat could fit the profile of a PPO and amongst the changes proposed comes the following recommendation:

Improved information sharing requirements between agencies.

Further into the report, one of the requirements the establishment should attend to is stated as follows:

Provide the police with intelligence gathered on a PPO while in prison (for example information about criminal contacts which may have been maintained while the PPO has been in prison, or offending during sentence). This information must be provided through the normal police liaison officer network, using the appropriate security information report (SIR) system.

It is just one requirement in a broader framework but it is an insight into how agencies aim to liaise so that persistent offenders can be targeted and steps can be taken to manage any risk they present.

In an ideal world of course, information gathering and sharing would be seamless and resources would be plentiful, so each insight could be followed up. But in reality, assessments have to be made all the time as thousands upon thousands of prisoners are released. Some represent a bigger risk than others and, whatever the rights or wrongs, certain offenders have to take priority over others.

Take Raoul Moat. He was a man known to the police but this was his first prison term. Some of his prior offences included driving away from a petrol forecourt without paying. Other more serious charges, including one of conspiracy to murder ten years earlier, had been dismissed. He had served a little over two months in prison, and his history of offending was not as prolific as that of others he would have served time with.

Whilst a Security Information Report was being put together about Moat, he was making his own preparations. A number of rumours were circulating. Moat had made threats against his ex and he had made remarks about his ex-mother-in-law (or, more accurately, mother of his ex-partner). Perhaps it was all bluster but maybe, this time, he would act on his frustrations and take it out on those closest to him. Perhaps he no longer feared prison and would risk being caught rather than let his ex believe that she could get away with dumping him and taking up relations with a police officer.

His future was uncertain and Sam's decision to end things made it even more so. He was in pain and he was brooding, and as he stepped into the summer air outside the prison, his thoughts were whirling and clicking into place. It was a tough time. He'd known tough times before, but now the landscape seemed different. Something had changed in him. Perhaps facing facts made him lock down certain thoughts and distil others. Look at the facts, he pondered to himself. He listed these on his Facebook page on the night of his release.

Just got out of jail, I've lost everything, my business, my property and to top it all off my lass of six years has gone off with someone else. I'm not 21 and I can't rebuild my life. Watch and see what happens.'

Perhaps there were those who doubted him. Soon, very soon, no one would doubt what Raoul Moat was capable of ever again.

CHAPTER TWO
1973

Newcastle's West End has known its share of problems. The city as a whole has been in an inexorable economic decline for decades, ever since the collapse of the heavy industries that forged so much of its identity, a proud heritage based on shipping, steel and coal.

There have of course been any number of initiatives to try and halt the decline and rebuild its economy and, as with much of the rest of the country, employment, where it has been created has been in the retail and service sectors. It's a far cry from its male-dominated blue-collar past, but times change and communities have to find a way to adapt.

The West End is called that because of its geography alone, standing as it does to the west of the city centre and stretching for about four miles to the A1. In many ways it is unremarkable: outlying towns were gradually absorbed by the city as it grew rapidly during the Industrial Revolution and now its residential streets look like many others, dominated by pre-war terraces and social housing built after the bombs stopped falling.

By the 1970s, the West End was at a crossroads although its residents were perhaps unaware of the drastic changes these would bring to the area. It was the start of de-industrialisation, the Vickers plant at Scotswood closed down and was followed by that of Elswick. The economic base that had underpinned the community was disappearing. With Vickers gone, others began to fail – engineering companies, components factories and metal spinners. The firms that provided decent wages and apprenticeships closed and nothing comparable was to take their place. Even when BAE systems opened a new plant in the 1980s, it employed 450 at its Scotswood site, compared to the 25,000 that had been working there at its height. It was truly the end of an era.

Unemployment numbers rose sharply, as did deprivation, and many people began to move out of the area, leaving houses unsold and boarded up. A great many of the 'slum terraces' had been demolished in the 1960s, and in the 1970s council estates took their place. Despite a number of initiatives, both on a large and small scale, none had any serious impact on the levels of poverty in the West End.

It was an area in decline. Population fell as those who could leave moved away and for those who stayed, ill-health was rife, educational attainment was poor, and jobs were scarce. It was into this declining community that Raoul Thomas Moat was born. This was not his mother, Josephine's, first child – she had already given birth to a son three years earlier. She named her first-born Angus, but was not in contact with his father or the father of her newborn second son.

Raoul is not a common first name but Josephine was not deterred by the locality's somewhat unimaginative expectations. Her family weren't originally from the West End and her maternal ancestors had once made their fortune in commerce. Much of that was a memory by the time Josephine's mother Margaret came to marry Thomas Moat. Raoul's mother was the youngest of three daughters and, like many young women growing up in the 1960s, she had adopted a much less constrained outlook on what she could do with her life in comparison with her mother's generation.

Josephine sought work as a draughtswoman, creating detailed technical drawings, something again which marked her out as different from many of her contemporaries: women who took part-time or unskilled jobs in order to work around their commitments as wives and mothers first, and wage earners second.

When Josephine was due to give birth to Angus in 1970, she was living with her parents. Neither they nor her sisters knew who the child's father was and she made the firm decision not to tell them. She was no longer a child, she was in her early twenties, and so there was little the family could do but accept her decision and support her as best they could.

Being a lone parent in 1970 carried a good deal more of a social stigma than it does today, only 40 years later. The word 'bastard' was a very hurtful insult for any child to have to bear but Josephine was undeterred and prepared to continue to work and to carry on with her life.

Some may have viewed this as a bold decision but, on the whole, this was a community that had many other concerns to preoccupy it. The West End was becoming notorious. Much of its 'lawless' reputation was an exaggeration but its rundown appearance, its empty and derelict houses, and abandoned industrial wastelands did little to alter perceptions. And besides, there were some episodes in its recent past that would forever associate the area with the worst of human tragedies.

Just two years before Angus was born, Mary Bell was arrested and later convicted for the manslaughter of two boys, four-year-old Martin Brown and three-year-old Brian Howe. Mary had grown up in and around the streets of Scotswood. Her mother was a prostitute and Mary had been severely abused, she would later claim, by both her mother and her mother's clients. She did not know who her father was and by the age of ten, she was a traumatised and troubled girl and it was the expression of her disturbed state of mind that would bring terrible consequences.

It was the day before Mary's eleventh birthday, 25 May 1968, when she found four-year-old Martin out playing. It wasn't until later that afternoon that his body was found in a boarded-up house by three other boys out looking for scraps to salvage. At the time, Martin's death was viewed as a possible accident and an open verdict was returned, but local residents were distraught and demanded that something should be done about the dangerous and derelict houses in the area. Indications that the young boy had been strangled were missed.

Just two months later, Mary and a friend Norma, an older girl but one very much in Mary's thrall, lured three-year-old Brian Howe onto some waste ground. Norma later confessed that she saw Mary asphyxiate Brian and that her attempts to pull Mary off the boy failed. She later returned with Mary to where Brian's body was hidden. Mary had brought with her a pair of scissors and a razor blade. The eleven-year-old carved the letter 'M' onto Brian's stomach and cut away some of his hair.

A month later the police had linked the two murders and the two girls were taken away to the West End police station and the trial was held in December of that year.

Norma was acquitted but Mary was convicted and sentenced to an indefinite sentence of imprisonment. She was eventually released in 1980 and her story hit the headlines once more when she collaborated on producing a book with the writer Gitta Sereny, a journalist who had covered the original trial.

In *Cries Unheard*, Bell revisited her childhood trauma and attempted to understand what drove her to do such appalling acts. One of the most revealing moments came when she described what she felt when she strangled another child:

'I'm not angry. It isn't a feeling... it is a void that comes... it's an abyss... it's beyond rage, beyond pain, it's a draining of feeling.'

This chilling absence of feeling, a release from feeling in fact, is characteristic of abused children who grow up to become abusers. Children who have suffered are at risk of maturing into young adults who find release only when inflicting pain on others.

At the time of Mary Bell's conviction she was described as displaying signs of psychopathology. To the residents of the West End she was seen as a monster. 'Mary Bell, Mary Bell, there's a place for you in hell', became a childhood rhyme and her name became a byword for something evil, something that could stalk and prey on children, a figure in the shadows like any other bogeyman.

Raoul Moat would have come to know the name – every child in the area did. There were some who believed she was born evil but as time moved on, more who wondered how much her environment shaped her, and in particular, the destructive role played by her mother, Betty Bell.

Neglect in childhood can have devastating consequences on the way a child develops, particularly the child's ability to form emotional bonds and show empathy for others. It is an issue that goes far beyond failing to provide food or clothing, it also encompasses the impact of emotional neglect.

Very often, if a primary carer is unable to provide loving and consistent emotional care for a child, the damage can be far reaching. It may be a temporary state such as postnatal depression and therefore can be overcome, and long-term difficulties can be avoided. But if a primary carer has an ongoing mental illness, the obstacles can be far harder to navigate, as Josephine's sons were to find.

Raoul's mother's surviving son, Angus, has spoken to the press of the difficulties he faced growing up. He has characterised his mother as someone who failed him and his brother. He said: 'Our mother was selfish. Without getting all dewy-eyed about it, we had a terrible childhood. My mother is not a very nice person.'

Every unhappy family is beset with anger and accusation and it is impossible to ever find the truth of what has gone on behind closed doors. No two accounts of what happened will match up and as time moves on, the past becomes ever more distorted by memory and regret. What is known is that Raoul and his brother were in large part raised by their maternal grandmother. Angus has said that his mother's presence was erratic and that she was absent for periods of time, although he accepts that her diagnosis as someone who was suffering with a bipolar disorder accounted for her spells in hospital.

Bipolar disorder, once known as manic depression, can be a challenge for any family. Children can witness a parent stare absently in a trance-like state for hours, or find them possessed by excessive energy, making plans that are hopelessly impractical and even running up serious debt as they pursue them. Not knowing what state a parent will be in each day, whether high and excitable or low and depressed, can cause stress and ongoing upset in a child. The youngster then might blame him or herself for the illness and internalise a lot of anguish, and the impossibility of distracting their parent and gaining much needed attention, can be the root of additional problems.

Not all children with a bipolar parent suffer, but many do. Looking at the bright and bonny pictures of Raoul as a baby, it is easy to imagine that he was a boy with everything to look forward to. But Angus has spoken of the difficulties his younger brother faced, saying: 'My mum was absent a lot of the time in mental hospitals. And often at home she was knocked out on medication. So you basically got a zombie or an absent mother.

'It's not a good position to be in. My grandma had to be there for us – and she was. She did a very good job.'

Having a stable and consistent influence in the life of any child that has an absent parent is essential if a young person is to thrive, but even with his grandmother's steady influence Angus has said that he struggled, particular with anger. He said: 'Yeah, it made me angry. I'm always angry. I'm still angry. Just not as angry as Raoul.'

How boys learn to mitigate their anger has been the subject of a number of studies and the impact of parenting in the early-years cannot be overlooked. It is believed that if boys do not receive enough consistent care and attention that the areas of the brain that process empathy and self-control can be damaged. It can affect the amygdalae, the part of the brain that processes memories that are connected to emotional events; and if the child has not learned that their needs are met, it can lead to an oversensitive reaction to stress.

Emotional neglect has also been linked to the fall in the production of the hormone serotonin that induces calm, whilst the production of corticosterone, the stress hormone, is increased. Taking all these factors into account, neglect in the early years can mean that some boys find it harder to develop empathy and have less control over their violent impulses when they encounter stress.

The plump baby smiling out in the Moat family album would grow up to find that his mother could not always provide him with the care he wanted and he would enter school knowing that he was one of the very few who did not have a father.

Angus helped. Being three years older, he was someone Raoul looked up to and would follow around his grandmother's house, and, unlike many brothers, Angus was happy to spend time with his young brother and the two quickly became inseparable. They looked different: perhaps not surprisingly, Angus had brown locks like his mother whilst Raoul had a shock of red hair. Physically the one thing they shared was their eye colour – both had bright blue eyes.

From the very start, as soon as he was able to, Raoul liked to spend time outside. He was at his happiest in the garden, looking under stones to find bugs, and he'd watch with fascination as insects and spiders crawled around. Sometimes he would even put them in his pocket, as if to keep them for later inspection. He was gentle, an inquisitive soul.

Come washing day, it wasn't uncommon to find Raoul's pockets filled with stones, leaves and anything else that caught his eye as he explored the garden. In that way, he was just like any other boy and yet his grandmother Margaret knew that when it was time to start school, he would not be regarded and accepted in the same way as the other boys would.

There was his name for a start. Raoul is uncommon now and was virtually unheard of in the mid 1970s. It is a

French version of the name Ralph and its roots are in Old Norse, meaning 'wolf counsel'. Josephine would hint at one stage to her youngest son that his father was French but it isn't possible to know if this was true or not. As it stood, no one would know how to spell his name and many would struggle with its pronunciation. Having an unusual first name is increasingly fashionable today, but 30 years ago it was more likely to guarantee that other children would find it something to mock rather than admire.

Angus was a name that wasn't common but at least it was recognisably Scottish and a great many people on Tyneside have Scottish ancestry. Yet even Angus found that his name would be played on and 'Angry Angus' and 'Anguish' would become two of the nicknames he'd become known by.

Anger. Even from the start it seemed that the two Moat boys would not be able to escape the effects of anger. Anger at an absent mother, anger at the void she left by not allowing them to know who their fathers were, anger that their ageing grandmother was the only consistent presence in their lives, and anger that others knew as much about their history as they did.

It is hard to keep any secrets in a tightknit community such as that of the West End. This may have been a community suffering economically and socially but that did not stem the persistent and ever-present interest that everyone had in everyone else's business; in fact, as family units started to break down and broken homes and absent fathers became more common, it could even intensify it. In Raoul's family there was a 'mad' mother and two 'bastard' boys.

Margaret would lie awake at night and wonder what would happen to her two beloved grandsons. Her boys were always together and in a favourite image, Raoul's first school photograph, they sat shoulder-to-shoulder with beaming smiles. She prayed that all her affection and care would be enough, that it would anchor them both. They'd had a tough start it was true but then so do many people who subsequently turn out perfectly all right.

Margaret had little idea of what lay ahead, of what would come to pass that would mean that two once inseparable brothers would spiral away from one another and onto very different paths.

CHAPTER THREE
IT BEGINS
FRIDAY 2 JULY

I wanted more, but I didn't know what.
– from Raoul Moat's letters

The drive is short, under half an hour, once you leave Durham prison and head towards the A1 and it doesn't take long before the signposts for Gateshead and Newcastle appear. It is a journey just shy of 17 miles but one long enough for Moat to have pondered again what lay before him. He would meet up with friends: he would need to as he had nowhere else to go.

There are only so many details that can be written about at present, since the investigation into what happened in the hours after Moat's release is still ongoing. The police would come to suspect that the ex-prisoner received help from some of his acquaintances, but it is yet to be determined if others were caught up in the bloody events. Anything that is written now cannot be seen to prejudice future trials, therefore journalists have to tread carefully when setting out what they know and what they have been told.

What can be said is that in the first 12 hours after Moat's release, there was a strange sense of unreality to all that the man did and the steps he took to enact his warped plan of action. Raoul himself was aware of how his rage could alter him. He would write: *'It's like the Hulk, it takes over and it's more than anger and it happens only when I'm hurt, and this time I was really hurt.'*

As most people know, *The Incredible Hulk* was the fictitious alter ego of Marvel Comic's scientist Bruce Banner. It is safe to say that the character's appeal isn't the accident in the laboratory with the Gamma bomb, but the mild-mannered Dr Banner's transformation into a raging humanoid beast. It is a transformation that only occurs once Banner is distraught either through grief, anger or more potently, both. To quote the big green man, 'The madder Hulk gets, the stronger Hulk gets.'

The character had particular resonance with its audience, boys and young men, and the fantasy that rage can be transformative has its attractions. The conceit is that if cornered by difficult emotions and situations, smashing your way out with superhuman strength and endurance is essentially blameless because the character is transformed (and later remorseful, calm and worthy of sympathy once more).

That is not to overstate the impact the comic or TV series that aired in the late 1970s had on Raoul but it is interesting as a motif, shorthand to explain that a man can be transformed when pushed to an extreme and emotional state of mind. Rage takes over.

There can be little doubt that Moat had, however, moved beyond anger and into thoughts of revenge on the day of his release. He was meeting and facing friends with his life in disarray. He'd lost custody of his daughters from an earlier relationship and, as a result, it was unlikely that he'd be able to keep the family home social services had allocated to him. Now, with Sam's visit, it was clear that he was in danger of losing access to his youngest daughter.

Losing a girlfriend can be heartbreaking but when children are involved, the fallout can be far greater, more destructive, and, for many men, an emotional firestorm. The last decade has seen the rise of fathers' rights campaign groups, a response to what many male parents have seen as an unfair bias in family courts. Although there are a number of groups, and a number of controversies, broadly speaking, campaigners would like to see parity of rights for fathers to see their children, for family courts to become 'open' and for courts to move away from the assumption that the primary carer should be the mother in all instances.

Needless to say, the issues the groups raise are far from straightforward. Whilst there was huge frustration that family courts were 'closed', it was done so as to protect the identity of children in often traumatic cases. When reporting restrictions were lifted in 2009, still with caveats that the identity of vulnerable children be protected, it became clear just how fraught some of the cases the courts have to deal with are.

On the month that restrictions were lifted, reporters attended a session where a council were petitioning to remove a four-year-old boy and a baby into care. There had been suspicion that abuse had occurred and social services had difficulty tracking the family as they moved from borough to borough. This was a far from straightforward case as it became clear that the young mother was the stepdaughter of the man who became the father of her children. Despite advice that she should break off relations, and attempts to do so, she admitted to still being in love with her stepfather.

It is these complex family issues that the courts find themselves faced with and it is almost impossible to reach decisions that will satisfy all those involved. Practical arrangements can be made but that can barely begin to accommodate the often fraught emotional needs and can, in some instances, inadvertently exacerbate them. A court's ruling can be read as inflexible and absolute, a judgement of your worth as a parent.

The child's needs are prioritised. In the first instance that means that the environment the child is placed in must be deemed to be safe and so where would that leave Moat? A man that now had not only served a custodial sentence, but whose alleged crime was for assault against a minor. Without Sam's active and positive decision to include him as part of their daughter's upbringing, he stood little chance of courts deciding that he should play a full parenting role in her life.

And no doubt Sam's decision to introduce another man to his daughter, another man taking his place in her bed and in her heart would have been like pouring petrol onto flames. This interloper could take his place in both his girlfriend's and his daughter's life – the latter was young enough to have few memories of who in fact her father was. How could Moat make sure that she would never forget him, never forget how much he loved her?

This toxic mix of self-pity, anger, frustration and remorse drove the anguished man to push his thinking into a tighter and tighter descent into destruction on that Friday afternoon. In allowing his wounded pride full expression, his options narrowed to one bleak endgame.

Amongst friends, he could have found shoulders to cry on, men to go out drinking with, when he could drown his sorrows with like-minded characters who'd agree that he'd been dealt a tough hand and that his ex didn't deserve him and who would try and assure him that things would get better. But Moat could not accept that this was the type of friendship he needed at that moment. He did not want pity. He had always cast himself as a self-sufficient man, someone who was capable, powerful even. Someone to look up to. A man of action, not words.

He was on the precipice but did not perhaps understand how close to the edge he was. As he hatched his plan, maybe he did not realise that by choosing to express his despair violently, everything that he claimed mattered in his life would be lost to him forever. All he could see was the need to do something, something big, and something that would show Sam that he wasn't to be messed around with and then discarded.

Moat wrote on his Facebook page and his anger and his despair is evident. He wrote:

Friday 11.21am Just got out the slammer to a totally fucked life.
11.32am Lost my business. Kids to s services. Gonna lose my home and lost my mrs of nearly 6 years to a copper. Like they havent fucked my life enough over the years.
11.37am Well she aint the lassy I thought she was. Cant win the kids, as police have fucked me over there too.
11.44am Mate this ones a hard knock. Its that whole rebuilding life from scratch thing. I aint 21 anymore.

11.54am Fucking strange how someone youve spent so long and treasured can turn on you like a pitbull. If Id fucked of with someone else id feel pretty shitty and definately twist the knife etc this ones a double hard knock.

12.22pm yea when its over its all a pile of chaos. How did a guy who had it all end up in this situation.

12.30pm Every action has an equal and opposite reaction, so if a lass can really love you and treat you right, then they can also swing the complete opposite way eventually.

As Moat made his preparations staff at Durham prison were completing theirs. Moat was no longer in their charge but following the requirements to flag up any concerns they may have had, the Security Information Report was completed, signed off and was making its way through official channels. The concern was simple enough – Moat had made threats about his ex, there was a risk that he could seek to harm her.

Again that brings us to a point where ongoing investigations limit what can be said here. It is known that the Security Information Report reached Northumbria police and it would be the temporary Chief Constable Sue Sim who would come to say as much. Whether that information was acted on as fast as it can reasonably be expected is open to conjecture. More importantly it is subject to an Independent Police Complaints Commission (IPCC) investigation. That means that contempt of court again becomes an issue; nothing that goes on record can be seen to prejudice proceedings.

So to tread carefully, beyond an acknowledgement that the Security Information Report was received, nothing more can be stated and it is interesting to note that IPCC investigations can take as long as two years before they reach their conclusion.

Off the record however, the police have spoken about the practical assessments that have to be taken when reports are received. It is worth remembering that the high numbers of those released from prisons each year will mean that an evaluation as to who poses an immediate risk is inevitable. Looking into the record of past offending is one approach: those with a long history of convictions for violence against others will top the list of those in need of monitoring.

The question of police resources is pertinent and not quite as straightforward as it at first appears. Despite year-on-year increases in police budgets and the recruitment of additional officers, Sir Denis O'Connor, HM Chief Inspector of Constabulary, announced in July 2010 that an average of only 11 per cent of officers and police community support officers (PCSOs) are able to meet frontline demands. In his role as police watchdog, he also stated that in some forces only six in every hundred officers are on a duty visible to the public during peak Friday night hours. So with greater numbers than ever, now standing at over 140,000 officers, as well as bigger budgets, how is it possible that the officers aren't visible and available in numbers?

As a former Met assistant commissioner, Sir Denis understands more about modern policing than most and he blames the low availability on a number of factors. He highlighted the reliance forces now have on PCSOs, who are an essential resource but do not continue their duties after 8pm. Shift patterns will also account for a large percentage of officers 'not available' but Sir Denis points to other trends in policing that are significant, namely risk management and bureaucracy.

Complaints about the time spent attending to paperwork are not new. In fact, two years before Sir Denis's report, The Home Office commissioned Sir Ronnie Flanagan to report into the future of policing so as to find ways of cutting bureaucracy. He warned that officers were being overburdened with red tape and noted that each officer could end up spending half their shift dealing with the process of arrest and detention, even if an offence is minor.

The paper trail is, however, a necessity, should a case come to court. Crown lawyers know that the defendant's legal representatives are adept at pulling cases apart if processes aren't followed clearly and diligently and cases can quickly collapse if the police can be shown to have failed to account for every detail.

The tension between effective frontline policing and the demands of case load management means that the assessment as to what has to be prioritised becomes inevitable.

As a rule, repeat and violent offenders receive longer sentences and that will mean access to the probation service and a stricter list of conditions once they are released. But Moat fell between the cracks. He was neither a long-term prisoner nor a man with a record of the worst and most serious of offences. He was known to the police but not as the totally different man he was fast becoming on that Friday: a brutal and calculating killer.

Did he recognise that man in himself? If there was a final step to take towards the transformation, it was a physical one. Moat shaved his hair. This was far more than a simple issue of disguise, after all, he was not being sought at this point – the manhunt would begin later. And even if he expected to go on the run, a Mohican haircut has to be one of the few grooming styles that can guarantee to attract attention, rather than allowing you to blend with the crowd. No, this was Moat going to war, and the iconography he chose is revealing.

Travis Bickle isn't a name that at first sight inspires fear but it was well chosen by Paul Schrader, the writer of *Taxi Driver*.

If the Hulk appealed to juveniles, Travis spoke to the angry and alienated man. Martin Scorsese's 1976 film may not have had immediate box-office appeal but it has gone on to become a revered classic and of course it was instrumental in launching the career of Robert De Niro. The actor gave perfect expression to the frustrated and misunderstood Bickle, a lonely ex-Marine and a man who saw himself swimming against a tide of all that was wrong in society.

But it is Bickle's decision to act that proved to be the most compelling aspect of the mind of this disintegrating man. Armed and possessed of a new sense of purpose, he shaves his head into the distinctive Mohican and acts out his new persona in front of a mirror in his room. Looking into the glass he is lost in a fantasy where an imaginary and unfeeling foe challenges him. In one of the most memorable scenes yet produced on celluloid he asks:

'You talkin' to me? You talkin' to me? You talkin' to me? Then who the hell else are you talkin' to? You talkin' to me? Well I'm the only one here. Who the fuck do you think you're talking to?'

In a fluid motion, the gun he has concealed on a sliding mechanism of his own creation slides into his hand as he enacts the role of a mild-mannered man who has been pushed and provoked and who is now ready to retaliate with terrible vengeance. So enacted, Bickle is ready to take his retribution to the street and track down and hunt his enemies.

This isn't Charles Bronson in *Death Wish* or Gregory Peck in *Cape Fear*, two characters who have a clear motive – an eye for an eye as their loved ones are killed or terrorised. *Taxi Driver* is far more haunting because Bickle's pain is real but misplaced, his enemies are everyone and no one, and the girl he kills for no longer recognises or understands him. His violence is futile and self-defeating. He is not the hero he believes himself to be, nor is he in control of the heroic persona he imagines will free him. All he leaves is carnage.

If there is a message that violence is futile and self-defeating, it wasn't the only one the film seemed to impart. *Taxi Driver* hit the headlines five years after its release when John Hinkley, Jr, attempted to kill US President Ronald Reagan. Hinkley was obsessed with Jodie Foster, an actor in the film, and in a moment where mental instability blurred the boundaries of reality and fantasy, he carried out his assassination attempt, an imitation of Bickle's attempt to kill a politician in the film.

Destruction, bloodshed, carnage – scenes, even imagined ones that we may recoil from – take on a dark attraction in the minds of those who are sufficiently disturbed. When all has been lost, and the pain is beyond containment, why should it not be made real for all to see and all to feel? Moat will have played with these dark thoughts, such as: *If I cannot have her, then no one will. If he thinks that he is the new man in her life, he did not reckon with me. If she thinks I can be cut out of her life so easily, she will live to regret it.*

With each fantasy came momentum. Moat standing over the man who took his girl from him, fear in Samantha's eyes and the eyes of her family. His thoughts would be: *They will learn to fear me and that I am all powerful, never to be messed with.* It was irrational, childlike almost in its reasoning, but utterly potent. The sense that this would be a road walked that could not be undone seemed beyond Moat's reasoning. All he could see was his pain and the desire to avenge.

Without overstating his transformation into a Bickle-like character, it is easy to see how he would identify with the creation. Bickle says: 'Listen you fuckers, you screwheads, here's a man who would not take it anymore, who would not let... a man who stood up against the scum, the cons, the dogs, the filth, the shit. Here is someone who stood up.'

This was exactly the mental terrain that Moat now inhabited. A man floored by circumstances beyond his control. Now he was standing up.

He'd lost weight over the last few weeks. His distress had suppressed his appetite and he had not been taking his usual array of supplements to maintain his shape and so was leaner than he had been for some years. Moat took pride in his physique. Now with his new haircut, he selected a bright orange tee shirt, a pair of dark jeans, white trainers and headed out to the Scotswood Road. Again, orange isn't the colour a man would choose if he was aiming to stay unnoticed. This was a statement colour, complete with Mohican. Standing at 6ft 3in, he felt ready to head back into the world and begin gathering the tools he would need for the job.

He would soon be in possession of a shotgun – how he acquired this has yet to be ascertained through the course of the ongoing investigation and the courts. In reality, Moat had existed on the fringes of various criminal networks for years, therefore getting a firearm would not pose much of a problem. The availability of firearms has been escalating for some time. By 2005 it was estimated that over four million guns were in circulation in the UK and, perhaps not surprisingly, between 1998 and 2008, the rate of gun crime had doubled. When it comes to the numbers of injuries, there were 1,760 gun-related injuries or deaths provisionally recorded for 2008/09, compared with 864 in 1998/99.

This has inevitably meant that the police have had to respond and Armed Response Units are part of policing teams across all forces. Moat would have known this; he would have known that firearms units have access to Heckler & Koch MP5 submachine guns, capable of firing 800 rounds a minute, and Glock semi-automatic pistols. But he was beyond caring. He knew that he would be able to do what he had planned and that it would be some time before they had any idea that he had started a war.

Raoul Moat headed to the hardware store B&Q on the Scotswood Road – he knew the DIY retailer well and it was only a few miles from his house in Fenham. There he picked up the items he'd need over the next few days. He'd already amassed other equipment, it was all part of his plan of action. If he had to go on the run, then so be it. He would keep busy until the time came, itemising what might be of use to him, playing out various scenarios and contingencies.

With the basics taken care of, all he had to do now was work out where Sam would be and when. That shouldn't prove too difficult. He knew where she liked to drink, who she'd talk to on a night out and, more pertinently, he had her parents' address. She'd be easy to track, easy to corner. He was calm, perhaps for the first time in a very long while.

CHAPTER FOUR
1977

The 'Building Schools for the Future' programme was the last government's flagship capital investment scheme and its aim was to either rebuild or renew all schools over the ensuing 15 years. The programme came to a juddering halt once the Coalition took power in May 2010 and cuts in public spending began in earnest, yet some schools had already been redeveloped and amongst that list was Stocksfield Avenue Primary in Fenham.

The school was moved to a new site and the impressive purpose-built constructions were completed in 2008. It was a new start for the school and no doubt Moat, a former pupil, will have noted how much had changed since his day. For better or for worse, schooling was different in the 1970s. It was 'chalk and talk', not the interactive, pupil-centred learning environments of today, where 'Maths days' can involve visits from a local celebrity, games, kite making and prizes.

Thirty years ago, school children sat in buildings mostly constructed by the Victorians, which were draughty and uninspiring. A lot of learning was still done by rote. Someone who was at school with Moat told a reporter that Raoul was laughed at because he could not even remember how to recite the two-times table. The future killer, it seemed, struggled to find his place in primary school.

It would be wrong to suggest that Moat wasn't bright but it is possible to imagine that he did not fit in easily into his new environment. Asthma would not have helped. Although a common childhood complaint today it was relatively rare then and marked him out, unhelpfully, as having yet another difference. Without even considering his issues at home, his red hair, wheezing and slight build made him an obvious candidate for bullying.

Clothing, too, was another problem. One ex-classmate said that he was teased and told that he looked like a tramp. Children can be cruel and a throwaway remark made my one child to another can often hit a sore point, as there may have been little extra money to spare at home. In the pecking order at school, sport, and in particular football, could have been his salvation, but he had no skill in that direction and so missed out. Raoul would never be the boy with the latest bike or game to show off to others so, all in all, the best he could expect was to keep his head down so as not to be noticed.

The late 1970s were a time of social change and upheaval. Whilst the Queen was celebrating her Silver Jubilee and people held street parties with flag waving and union jack bunting fluttering, the Sex Pistols were enjoying a hit with their iconoclastic hit 'God Save the Queen'. The single didn't make it to Number One in the hit parade but the rumour circulated that it was deliberately kept off the top spot. It was banned by the BBC, the institution at the time reflecting the outrage of Middle England.

The band was already notorious for swearing live on Bill Grundy's *Today* programme. Watching the footage, it is as if two worlds collided – the late 1950s-born disaffected youth mocking the generation that was raised pre-war. There was no respect for anything that Grundy represented and it seemed that all that was sober, traditional and restrained was under threat. The tabloids had a frenzy of indignation and shock with the *Daily Mirror* announcing that the incident as 'The Filth and the Fury'.

The fury was evident in the Sex Pistols' lyrics, young people latched onto 'God Save The Queen' as Lydon sneered that there was 'no future' for his emerging generation. He had a point. Britain was locked into an apparently unstoppable and serious spiral of economic decline and industrial unrest. In 1977, firefighters went on strike, asking for a 30 per cent pay increase and that kind of union demand was commonplace. By the following year, during what was described as 'The Winter of Discontent', car workers, refuse collectors, lorry drivers, railwaymen, nurses, ambulance and lorry drivers were on strike. Refuse started piling in the streets and the army was on standby should a state of emergency have to be called by the Callaghan administration.

With unemployment rising, the future for anyone growing up in Britain did look bleak. Younger children like Moat will not have been aware of the issues in any detail but the sense that this was a community, and a part of the country in decline, was all pervasive.

For Raoul Moat, school could have offered a positive escape but that wasn't to be. Home, then, should have been a refuge but matters were about to take a turn for the worse. Josephine suffered a number of episodes and Angus Moat remembers an occasion when his mother spoke in an intense and garbled way about religion, telling him and Raoul that they were the 'chosen people' and that the boys were 'going to be Princes' and that they were not to be sad 'because the devil doesn't want to you to be sad'.

Manic episodes, if indeed this was one, can be upsetting

for anyone to witness and particularly disturbing for a child. Angus can remember crying, and feelings of distress are hard to dismiss when a parent is in a manic state. Children have an innate belief that adults tell the truth and so the more alarming the claims, the more frightening they are to hear.

Bipolar can induce psychotic extremes, when mania strikes it can exceed the sense of general elation and cause the sufferer to believe that they have special powers or are charged with a mission. It can also induce hallucinations. Stress can provoke episodes of either depression or mania in the sufferer and the condition has a high rate of recurrence. If untreated, approximately 15 per cent of sufferers commit suicide.

It is a life-long disease and runs in families and it is thought that a child will have a 25 per cent chance of developing a mood disorder if a parent is bipolar. If both parents are bipolar, the risk that a child will develop a mood disorder rises to between 50 and 75 per cent. The Moat brothers of course, had no idea if their biological fathers were mentally healthy or not.

Not enough is known as to what triggers bipolar disorders but some research suggests that it is associated with abnormal brain levels of serotonin, dopamine and norepinephrine: hormones that regulate stress and feelings of wellbeing.

Bipolar affects each sufferer to a varying degree and, of

course, some families cope better than others. The duration of the depressive and manic episodes differ too but what is alarming is that manic episodes usually begin abruptly and can last for between two weeks and five months. Depressive episodes tend to last longer, commonly for six months, though rarely for more than a year but to a child growing up in an environment with a parent suffering from the condition, such periods of time will seem interminable.

People suffering from bipolar have to take lithium and often antipsychotic drugs indefinitely, and these drugs can suppress episodes. But as mania can quickly escalate there is a risk that it will destroy a sufferer's career or reputation, which is usually why doctors will hospitalise out-of-control patients before they 'lose everything'. In a manic state, people have been known to waste thousands of pounds chasing ideas and impulses. Likewise, severely depressed and suicidal patients often require hospitalisation to save their lives.

Bipolar disorder becomes evident commonly at around the age of 20 and yet many sufferers report that they felt the onset of the illness before the age of 13. Interestingly, research has also shown that the children of parents with bipolar who grow to have the condition themselves have an earlier onset of the illness. It has been called the 'anticipation effect' and the children in question also report a greater number of episodes when compared to their parents.

Furthermore, these adults with earlier onset may have diminished response to drug therapy and are more likely to be at risk of attempting suicide. An early diagnosis of developing bipolar disorder is far from clear but symptoms in children older than five years old include withdrawal, a change in appetite, unexplained gastric complaints, mood elevation and committing violent and destructive acts.

As Raoul grew, there would be incidents that he was said to be involved in that could suggest that he was at the outset of a bipolar disorder developing. Perhaps there is no truth to them and perhaps they have been exaggerated – such as the time that he allegedly burnt down a corner shop. It was said that he deliberately set fire to cardboard boxes at the back of the premises and that it was subsequently destroyed, and that this was just one example of how destructive he could be.

Another incident involved a cat. It was said that he was going to throw a cat off a balcony but that other boys who knew him from school tried to stop him. He threw it anyway, claiming that cats always land on their feet, but then he was said to have slammed the cat into the ground, breaking its back.

Both arson and misuse of animals are classic, in fact textbook, signs of developing psychosis in childhood. Studies carried out by forensic psychologists who have surveyed serial and multiple killers show time and time again the patterns that emerge in childhood. Children who have been severely mistreated, and commonly that includes prolonged sexual as well as physical and emotional abuse, can begin to fantasise about relocating their internal pain onto an external object.

Dr Deborah Schurman-Kauflin has interviewed serial killers at length. They agreed to talk to her on the understanding that they would remain anonymous. She put together a study of the formative experiences in the lives of these killers and a strikingly similar series of events were shared across the seven incarcerated killers who agreed to be interviewed.

Neglect and abuse in childhood occurred in all cases and as the early years passed, the children had all mistreated animals. Here is what one convicted killer said about attacking a dog:

'No one could see what I was doing. I always made sure there was no one to see what I was doing. And I took the clothes line and I tied his back legs together so there was nowhere he could go. I picked up a stick and whacked him upside his head, and finally that little shit stopped yipping, and I kept hitting him with sticks and rocks until he cried…the more he cried, the more I liked it. It was like, hey, finally, something else feels like I do. Let something else suffer for a change.'

All of the respondents confessed that it felt good to see something else suffer but each also recorded that they felt a curiosity, a wonder that they created death. It was real, it was a convincing way to show that they had taken back power and were in control of it.

The difficulty is that the incidents of violence and destructive behaviour that were given to a tabloid news reporter seem almost too neat. If Moat became a 'monster', then it becomes too easy to imagine a narrative whereby the boy-Moat displays early psychotic behaviour. Whether this was true or not or simply a tale that became embellished in the retelling can become lost in the desire to create a simple sequence of events that culminated in Moat raising a shotgun and firing. But lives aren't led that way, cause does not always follow effect in the human character. Early childhood experiences, genetic factors and environment do shape a young person's character, but not always in the same way in every case.

Besides, others who knew Moat when he was a boy do not recognise the picture of him as a child who was willfully cruel to animals. His brother and mother have both spoken about the younger Raoul being a nature lover, a lad who cared for his two cats Smokie and Fifi, and that if one characteristic was especially noticeable in his childhood it was his sensitivity.

Of course, no two people will recall events in exactly the same way; each of us takes different meaning from shared occurrences and memories can be deceptive. Yet it does not seem to be the case that Moat was well-known as the boy who terrorised his neighbours and was branded 'mad and dangerous'. He joined the Scouts and later the Army Cadets but was not singled out as a dangerous troublemaker. If he was picked on for the differences in his background, he learned to embellish rather than deny that his father was unknown to him. He said that he'd been born in France, that he lived there until school age on a large farm with his father until his parents went their separate ways. It must have helped him deflect any negative remarks his classmates might have made. Fellow pupils at Stocksfield Avenue Primary School have expressed shock that the boy that they knew was to become a killer who was notorious throughout the country. And a picture of him with his classmates suggests nothing: he smiles broadly into the camera just as his peers do, standing or sitting in their neat rows. But of course behind the innocent facade something wasn't right. Something buried deeper in his psyche would mean that thirty years later, he would respond to personal crises with devastating violence.

Another view put forward is that Moat was developing another behavioural disorder: Narcissistic Personality Disorder. This is a condition characterised by a need for admiration, extreme self-involvement, and lack of empathy for others. Difficulties managing self-worth are thought to make individuals with the condition oversensitive to criticism or failure. Any perceived criticism provokes feelings of humiliation and can result in rage and an angry counterattack.

The condition isn't understood as clearly as other more

documented disorders such as bipolar, and suspected causes of the defect include both an overindulgent mother or father and unpredictable and unreliable parenting. So it seems that Narcissistic Personality Disorder can be incubated by parents that place too high a regard on their child as well as those who are negligent and detached. Yet rather than viewing indulgent or negligent parenting as two ends of a spectrum, it is easy to imagine that they can produce a similar result. In both instances, the emotional needs of the child are secondary to the needs or deficiencies of the parent and this can have a significant and negative impact on childhood development. It can undermine the child's ability to form bonds of trust with others as they reach maturity.

Children with the condition eventually begin to see themselves as having a separate identity from their parents and they begin to start processing parental behaviour with a degree of detachment. Angus Moat has spoken about the moment he began to remove himself from his mother's more disruptive behaviour and it occurred at a key time in Raoul's life – he was around seven years old.

The older Moat son recalls that it was during one of Josephine's manic episodes, and she had once more begun to talk in an extreme way, using religious imagery. On this occasion, Angus does not remember fear or confusion, he recalls thinking 'you are full of shit.' It was a remarkable departure from the fear and upset of two years earlier and indicative of the fact that children quickly learn to become emotionally defensive and even closed off from disturbing events.

Whatever the truth of the incident, bipolar is a recognised illness and it would be unfair to ask sufferers to be accountable for their behaviour during episodes. Nevertheless, growing up in the company of a bipolar illness sufferer will affect some children and Angus has stressed that despite the efforts of his grandmother, the childhood he and his brother shared was traumatic.

Learning that a parent cannot give unqualified love and support is not a lesson that is learned once but one that is repeated time and time again. Even if a child builds a psychological wall around themselves, it is a construct that then damages their chances of forging meaningful bonds later in life. Questions about trust become all consuming, such as: can I trust this person? Will they always be there for me? Are they worthy of my love? Am I worthy of theirs?

Whilst growing up, the issues are chiefly ones of survival; for example, how can I stop this person hurting me? Anger is a common emotion and is one route to forging a sense of separation. Although rage has its uses in protecting a sense of self, if unchallenged and un-channelled, it can grow to become a destructive element in someone's psychological make-up. If that person feels undermined, threatened or disregarded, the emotional response can be explosive.

Raoul still had his brother and his grandmother and also his uncle Charlie, Josephine's brother-in-law, who was a positive male role model. But over the course of his short life, he had come to know that those closest to him could be absent, neglectful and unstable. He did not have a father and he was reaching his teens, a time when he needed to understand his place in society. What did the world have in store for him? He may not have had the easiest of starts in life but that is the case for a lot of people and a great many go on to use their pasts to fuel their ambitions for the future. We don't have to be defined by our pasts – but how far can we outrun them?

CHAPTER FIVE
CONTROL
SATURDAY 3 JULY

*I've slept one hour per night for weeks now. It feels
like I'm watching a film, not real at all.*
– from Raoul Moat's letters

Friday night in Newcastle has traditionally been for many people a big night out. The town's reputation as a place where girls and boys party hard is no exaggeration – indeed having a 'cracking' night out is almost an entitlement in that part of the world.

Not that it differs too greatly from other northern towns, but generally speaking Newcastle is thought to have the highest estimated level of binge drinking in England. Friday nights see thousands out on the city's streets; the Bigg Market and The Gate entertainment complex attract the greatest numbers of revellers. But the atmosphere is positive; everyone is chasing a good time, not aggravation.

Where there is alcohol, however, trouble is never far away and the city council has gone to great lengths to try and improve safety at night. In partnership with the bars, the areas now have taxi marshals on patrol as well as street pastors to try and smooth over and pre-empt any flash points of disagreement and potential violence. The nighttime economy is now worth millions to the city, and as the economic decline of the 1970s and 1980s flattened out, it seemed that young professionals started to move back to the town centre and that leisure became one of the few economic sectors that had the potential to keep growing.

Raoul had been part of all that. In his role 'on the doors', he used to watch and supervise the crowds as they went into clubs and back out onto the streets. Raoul had loved 'the doors'.

This Friday, early in July, was no different than any other. The number of people out isn't really affected by the weather, which in turn is another part of Newcastle's reputation as a party town. Lasses will step out in skimpy outfits on a wet weekend in November just as they do on a warm evening in July. The *Daily Mail* was even prompted to run a feature highlighting research that suggested that northern women really don't feel the cold as they have 'thicker skin'; the suggestion was that further north, women eat 46 grams of saturated fat each day compared to the 33 grams consumed by women from the South East.

The north/south divide is alive and well, although researchers at Newcastle's International Centre for Life conceded that going out without a coat on a cold night is just as likely to be a cultural norm as it is a factor of being 'hardy'. That northern women like their finery, enjoy display, and aren't inclined to spend half the night worrying about finding a cloakroom, are perhaps factors that really dictate what women wear on a night out. Moat had his views. He was conscious of what women wore and particular about how his girlfriends presented themselves. He had been very particular about Sam: he liked her to look a certain way, as he had been very proud of her.

Now he knew in his heart of hearts that there would be no more Friday nights out; no more buzzes of anticipation, or the awareness of knowing that you'd be seen out and about with your glamorous girlfriend on your arm, a real man with a lot going for him. That was gone. It was all narrowing down to one place and one time. And that time would be tonight: a 'straightener'.

He'd spoken with Sam and he'd hated listening to her. She was firm about it being over between them and it was as if the Sam he knew, the Sam he needed, had gone. To Moat, this girlfriend had been all he had ever wanted and her decision to end their relationship and to drive him out of her and his daughter's life rendered every other option before him futile. A 'straightener' meant tackling this new man. Sam said it wasn't going to happen.

Moat had carried out his own research concerning his girlfriend's latest man. It was true that he was a karate instructor and a body builder and, evidently, he wasn't the kind of man Raoul could easily intimidate. Then there was all this talk about him being a policeman. Moat looked into that too. Sam saying that the guy was a police officer pushed every button. The aggrieved ex-lover felt that she should know instinctively that this knowledge made him feel bullied and hemmed in. He was sure that she knew how he felt himself to be persecuted by the police and that by saying that her boyfriend was a police officer, it was not an attempt to keep him away but was a remark designed to taunt and provoke him. How could she have known him so well and now expect him to just give up? He wrote: *Your mam and boyfriend don't really know me, but you do.*

He called Sam a few times that night, trying to talk to her, trying to see if she'd make it all stop. But she was out, in Gateshead, at a pub with her new boyfriend, and although she spoke to him on the phone, it made matters worse, not better. He could hear that noise and laughter of the crowd in the pub in the background and it was tipping him closer to the point of no return. The weight of his grief was too much to bear. He could no longer carry it, someone else had to. As he wrote to Sam: *You see, you can kill a person without ever physically harming them, you just make them harm themselves.*

If Sam didn't know that, now he'd have to show her.

The drive didn't take long, Sam's parents' home was only eight miles or so from Fenham. He knew that she would be heading back there after a night out with this new man, Chris Brown.

Sam had arranged for a babysitter to look after her daughter Chanel until morning and the plan had been that she would stay over at Chris's place, but after the calls from Moat, that now changed. Chris could see that Moat had upset Sam and so he suggested that he take her back to her parents' home instead. She agreed: she'd prefer to be near them and Chanel but she suggested that she should go back there alone. Although Raoul had been making threats against Chris, Sam sensed that he didn't know what her new boyfriend looked like and so if he stayed away from her family's home, he would be safe. Chris wouldn't hear of it. He wouldn't be happy unless he knew that he'd got her home safely and, besides, he wasn't the kind of man to hide just because an ex was being unreasonable. He'd take care of her, no matter what.

Chris wasn't from the North East, he'd arrived fairly

recently from his home in Slough to take up a new job, and although he'd not lived in the locality long, he'd quickly made good friends at the gym and was popular. He was easy-going and always made an effort with people, he had a ready smile, was quick-witted and good company. For Chris, meeting Sam had been a bonus. She had come to the gym a few times and they'd always have a laugh. They'd been out on a few dates and it was still early days but he thought they got on very well. He liked Sam and didn't like to see her upset about her ex.

In fact, it wasn't to her parents' house that they arrived just after midnight; they returned to Jackie's house, a friend of Sam's who lived in the house next door-but-one. Chanel was upstairs asleep and Sam's mum Lesley was up chatting with Jackie. They asked Chris in and all sat together in the front room to talk about the night. Chris wanted to make sure that Sam wasn't too worried about Moat. He stayed and chatted and made Sam laugh – it was the best way to distract her and make her feel that everything would be okay. Chris reasoned that of course Moat was upset, after all he'd only just got out of prison and, as the jealous type, he was likely to be feeling hard done by. It would all calm down over time.

Jackie's house was well kept, Raoul could see that. There was a porch built around the front door and to the right of that, flowerpots under the front-room window. It was easy for Moat to slip through the black wrought-iron gate and squat down under this window nursing the sawn-off shotgun. He heard their voices; he heard Sam laughing.

Raoul's ex-partner had decided to leave Chanel to sleep upstairs. She did think about carrying her next-door-but-one to her mum's house but thought it best not to disturb the little girl now since it was so late: it had gone 2.30am. This is how Sam described the next few minutes. It was time for Chris to leave; he had a busy day ahead of him and so made ready to depart. He could tell that Sam was happy again, that her mind was free of the worries that she'd had about Moat.

The couple walked to the door. Chris was on Sam's left and he kissed her goodbye just before they both stepped out into the night. As they walked towards the green at the front of the house, it took nothing, a matter of seconds, for Moat to jump up, aim, and then shoot Chris. Sam screamed out – the noise had been deafening and she felt the force of the gunshot. She knew Moat was the gunman even though her ex had not said a word.

Chris staggered forward and Raoul shot again, this time hitting him in the back. He fell, but did not yell out. Sam was screaming at Moat, unable to comprehend what was happening in front of her eyes. She ran to Chris and Moat slowly followed. The three were alone on the green. Sam turned to look at Moat and she saw something that made her blood run cold – there was no expression at all on

Moat's face. Nothing. She had seen his rage before, his anger, the way his features would contort as he lashed out. But now he was a blank, nothing registered on his face. Instinct told her that Moat would kill again. She cared not for herself but knew she had to protect her daughter Chanel — she was aware that Moat wanted to destroy everything in his wake.

Sam ran back towards the house and Moat again began to track her slowly. He stopped. The gun had another shell he could fire before he would need to reload it. He walked back to Chris and stood over him. He put more ammunition into the firearm, raised the barrel and shot him in the back of the head. Without a pause, he began busying himself with the gun once more. There was one more shell. This wasn't over.

His steps took him back to the house. He stood watching. The house was ablaze with light and commotion, in stark contrast to his motionless frame. Sam's mum had run upstairs, desperate to save her granddaughter. She picked the three-year-old up and ran to the attic entrance, pleading with her to hide and remain quiet.

The younger woman was trying to keep Moat out. She knew that none of them would survive if he got into the house but the keys were not in the lock: she could not lock the door. Jackie was in shock and struggled to marshal her thoughts. Where were the keys, she wondered? Before she could tell Sam, she saw her friend walk over to the window.

The young woman was looking at Chris, she could see that he was not moving. And as she stood framed in the bay window, it was all Moat needed. He raised the gun once more, took aim and fired.

The glass shattered. Sam had not even turned her head Moat's way; she had been looking beyond him and towards Chris. She had seen sparks from the shot from the corner of her eye but the pain at first did not register. Part of her understood that she had been shot and she called out to Jackie. And yet it was not pain that concentrated her mind but the fight for air. She could not breathe.

Jackie was in tears and desperately dragged her friend across the floor and into the kitchen, in the hope that she would then be beyond Moat's range. All he had to do was walk in, then they'd all be finished. Jackie bundled a white tablecloth onto her friend's stomach: the blood loss was immediate and horrifying. It was pumping out of Sam's shattered abdomen and arm. Jackie pleaded with Sam to be quiet, it was their only hope.

The door opened. But it wasn't Moat walking in, it was Sam's mother Lesley running out to confront Moat. She screamed: 'You shot my baby! Shoot me you bastard!' Lesley's husband Paul by now knew that something was terribly amiss. He came out of their home, two doors away, and he saw his wife outside with Moat. He chased after her and saw Moat with the gun aimed at her head. Like Sam, he too was struck by the absence of emotion in Moat's expression. He called out and it was as if Moat saw him for the first time. In this moment of doubt, Moat hesitated, then turned and ran. Paul gave chase but his wife's cries made him stop and run back to her and the house.

Sam was fighting for her life. Jackie was cradling her and sobbing. The kitchen was a scene of carnage. Blood was pooling around Sam, the white tablecloth was now red, and as Sam struggled for air, it did not seem possible that she would survive.

It was a neighbour that raised the alarm. He had heard the shots and then saw a man lying face down on the green. The police and paramedics were on the scene in minutes and the frantic effort to keep Sam alive began in earnest. She was rushed to Gateshead's Queen Elizabeth's Hospital and police began their work, cordoning off the scene. Chris Brown was pronounced dead and forensic work began as officers started to piece together an account of the night's events.

Raoul Moat was nowhere to be seen. Paul had called the killer on his mobile but it went to answer message. The words he left were stark: 'If you think that is being a man it's not.'

There was no question as to who the gunman was. Sam was in the operating theatre and would be there for some hours to come but the police had been told that Raoul Moat was the man who had shot Sam and her boyfriend.

Detective Superintendent Steve Howes of Northumbria Police would head the enquiry. He gave a brief statement to the press saying: 'I would like to stress that this is not a random attack and that the people involved are all known to each other. We believe the offender targeted his victims because of a grudge he held against them.' The police would not confirm what had caused the man's death, that would only come after a postmortem later that day, but they added that they 'believed death to be consistent with a gunshot wound.'

Initially, what had happened in Birtley appeared to be following an all-too-common outcome of domestic abuse. Moat had been violent towards his ex-partner Samantha Stobbart and she had chosen to end the relationship some time ago, possibly as long as a year earlier. But they had been in contact. The suspect, Moat, had called her repeatedly since his release from prison only two days before. It appeared that he had not accepted that she had ended the partnership and he was incensed to learn that she had begun a relationship with another man.

On average, two women are killed by a partner or ex-partner every week in the UK. The figures are stark. Forty-six of all female homicide victims compared to five per cent of male homicide victims are killed by current or former partners. And it is when they try to leave a violent relationship that they are at greatest risk.

Police forces across the UK have made determined efforts to reassess how victims of domestic abuse have been dealt with over the last 30 years. The notion that what happened behind closed doors was a 'domestic' issue and should remain largely unchallenged has been debunked. The damage that domestic abuse brings to the lives of victims and children in a relationship is now recognised as severe and debilitating and yet amongst the wider public not all are sympathetic to the victim. Ideas that 'some women ask for it', that it 'was just a slap' or that some women 'choose' violent partners, remain entrenched in the public psyche.

Despite the insistence that women subject men to domestic abuse, the fact remains that abusers are almost overwhelmingly male and the victims are female. Research into the issue revealed that 81 per cent of reported domestic violence cases were of female victims attacked by male perpetrators; eight per cent were male victims attacked by female perpetrators; four per cent were female victims attacked by female perpetrators, and seven per cent were male victims attacked by male perpetrators.

Highlighting the fact that men are more often than not abusers and not the abused does not suggest that men are inherently 'violent'. In fact, what it should do is force a broader examination of what we accept as a society. Women's Aid, the national domestic violence charity, states simply: 'Male privilege operates on an individual and societal level to maintain a situation of male dominance, where men have power over women and children.'

The statement continues: 'Perpetrators of domestic violence choose to behave abusively to get what they want and gain control.'

No matter the changes that society has been through since the war and the strides towards equality that women have taken, men are still expected to take charge and be in control. There continues to be a sense of male entitlement, men earn more than their female counterparts and even nowadays dominate boardrooms and government. But this isn't an argument about why women haven't broken through the 'glass ceiling'; it is an acknowledgement that if men are 'expected' to take charge, there can be a very high and negative price to pay for those who 'fail'.

There are men who, if they feel undermined and consider that their position is under threat, counteract with violence. This is not about losing control. On the contrary, the men who abuse partners, and often do the same to their children behind closed doors, are selective about who and when they abuse. Domestic violence, then, is about gaining control, not motivated by a lack of control. Abusers may snap and lash out in a moment of temper and later feel genuine remorse but what underpins their behaviour is a feeling of inadequacy. They are not 'real men'; what they see as 'transgressions' by either a wife or girlfriend, threaten their sense of control, and in order to impose their will they have to employ force.

As the enquiry team gathered witness statements concerning the Moat shootings, what had happened in the early hours of the morning appeared to be the action of an abuser who had set out to annihilate the woman he could no longer control. And it seemed as if her new partner had suffered the misfortune of being caught up in his retribution.

Later that day, the name Raoul Moat had been released by police. They warned the public not to approach him as he could be dangerous, but stressed that everyone involved in the incident had been linked to him. This had the effect of reassuring the community and Detective Superintendent Howes added: 'I would like to stress that this is not a random attack and that the people involved are all known to each other.'

In truth, it is rare for anyone outside the family setup to become a victim of a domestic abuser. The hope must have been that intelligence would quickly lead the police to Moat or that he would give himself up. He was known to them, he had had contact with the police on several occasions over the last few years, and so a list of the addresses he frequented and his associates could be compiled relatively quickly.

Yet it is interesting to note that when local journalists ran his name through their systems, fully expecting Moat to feature in previous stories that had run over the years, there was no trace of him. He was not a man with a string of high profile links to crime, nor had he received a number of convictions. In fact, the recent gaol term had been his first. He was a fairly ordinary man — certainly he was muscle-bound, but then if you walk around the nightclubs of the city on a Saturday night, muscular men are a common enough sight.

But Moat was nowhere to be found, at least not in those first few hours of the enquiry. Patience and diligence in police work are key, and a careful compilation and assessment of verifiable facts is what yields results. And if you talk off-record to detectives, with a little bit of luck, that moment of breakthrough might come that allows the team to close in on the suspect and know that they have all they need to build a case that is watertight.

If a little luck is what it takes, this case would become significant for its absence.

This was not the start of a single enquiry. This case was about to bring havoc to Northumbria and spark the largest British manhunt in recent memory. It had only just begun and it was far from over. Away from Birtley, Moat was brooding about the horror he had brought in the early hours of that morning. He had killed. In his mind, he was right to do so. He believed Sam had taunted him, and, in his mind, Brown had challenged him; in Moat's agitated state, he needed to 'fight back'. Of course, this wasn't a fight. This was an execution. He had eliminated the man who had taken his place in Sam's life.

And despite witnessing the result of his rage and the terrible fear and bloodshed that he had brought into the life of a woman he claimed to love, he wasn't ready to stop. He wanted more.

CHAPTER SIX
1986

As the decade moved on, Margaret Thatcher's government's plan for a radical shake-up of how Britain did business was at its height. Things were certainly changing, but not for everyone.

The American economist Milton Friedman was a leading inspiration. He did not believe that the government should attempt to micromanage the economy with a view to shaping society and, in fact, believed that attempts to do so would create greater difficulties. He had such little faith in central governments that he even quipped: 'If you put the federal government in charge of the Sahara Desert, in five years there'd be a shortage of sand.'

To Friedman and a great many others who were shaping government policies on both sides of the Atlantic in the late eighties, it was essential that business be freed up from regulation and that the market be allowed to conduct its business unfettered, as that was the most likely way to generate wealth and opportunities for all.

It was individuals who mattered, not government. In fact the only legitimate role for government was to ensure individual liberties. This was the antidote to Keynesian economics, the interventionist approach to government that had held sway since the Second World War. Friedman was unequivocal when he said: 'The greatest advances of civilisation, whether in architecture or painting, in science and literature, in industry or agriculture, have never come from centralised government.' And with that belief driving the heart of Margaret Thatcher and her party's outlook, the economic landscape was transformed.

State-owned business were privatised, regulations thought to constrict business freedoms junked, uneconomic industries were not to receive state support but had to either streamline or close. That a 'natural state of unemployment' would be an outcome was accepted as inevitable, but the belief was that 'trickle down economics' would eventually create opportunities for all those willing to work hard. This was to be a new way of doing business and it would mean a new dawn for Great Britain. Margaret Thatcher knew what she was up against and she was willing to take the fight to those she saw as standing in the way of progress.

Only two years earlier, the National Union of Miners (NUM) called a national strike and it was the start of a long and bitterly divisive year. Arthur Scargill had called for industrial action as a series of pit closures were announced and it was to become a battle between the new economic beliefs and the entrenched views of some in the union movement.

So much had changed from a decade earlier when the miners' strike of 1974 had received widespread support from other unions. Then, the country was plunged into power shortages and the Heath government was brought to its knees. Yet by 1984, there was no such consensus.

By not holding a national ballot, Scargill had miscalculated and not every NUM branch supported the action. Other key unions, such as the steelworkers, did not come out in support either and the striking miners were gradually isolated and worn down.

In areas of little support for the strike, South Derbyshire for example, only 11 per cent came out on strike and by the following year, that number had not changed. That compared differently with the North East, where the strike had received over 95 per cent support at the start of the strike but that figure fell to 60 per cent by its end. Miners' families suffered real hardship and the fact that a slow trickle of men were who returning to work caused rifts between families and neighbours, some of which are yet to heal.

The defeat was a huge blow to not just the NUM but the whole of the union movement. Times were changing. De-industrialised communities suffered most and were told that they would only be renewed once they embraced 'enterprise'. Yet this was a hollow promise, suitable perhaps as a model for the services sectors that were emerging in London and the south east but not actionable in the communities that had lost its heavy or manufacturing industries.

Dave Hopper was the NUM leader of the North-East during the strike and is still angry about what he sees as Margaret Thatcher's legacy. He said: 'She did more damage to our communities and people than the Luftwaffe. You look around our area now and there are not a lot of meaningful jobs, jobs that give people dignity and with which they can build up a family, buy a home and have security.'

Perhaps no one was fully aware of the extent that the loss of heavy industry would have on communities as a whole, not even the NUM. But it was significant that not all of the country suffered, because the late 1980s would prove a very different era for some. This was also the time when 'Loadsamoney' – the catchphrase used by Harry Enfield's comedy character, a plasterer with a Thames Valley accent – entered the language, and Enfield's creation, along with

Paul Whitehouse's complementary character, were stars of a sellout tour. This caricature of working-class greed was aggressively self-interested, considering the only thing that measured a man was his ability to make quick and easy money, or as 'Loadsamoney' would say: 'Look at my wad!'. Paid 'cash in hand', the character epitomised all that was newly liberated in this 'free' market. It is significant that he wasn't an investment banker; he was an ordinary working man, now released from the old constraints of unionised labour.

The old dynamics were dead and a great many were happy to see the previous notions go on the funeral pyre. This was an aggressive and individualistic new era and few people remember Enfield's other character, Geordie 'Bugger-all-money' half as well or with as much affection. Without the cash and the swaggering confidence of someone reaping the rewards of an economic boom, 'Bugger-all-money' was left with little left to define himself and so resorted to the northern hard-man stereotype, with sentiments such as: 'Loadsamoney, loads of bloody handbags more like, he's a typical soft southerner.'

It was fine for men looking for well-paid employment in the South East – for instance there was a strong and growing demand for housing and so construction and renovation projects offered plenty of opportunities for skilled labourers. But in areas where houses were being boarded up and equity in housing was flat or in decline, the chance to carve out your own 'wad' was harder to come by. The Employment Secretary Norman Tebbit had already told the unemployed to 'get on their bikes and look for work' but many had to go further afield than England, as the popular TV series *Auf Wiedersehen Pet,* about British construction workers on a German building site, illustrated. Workers had to be flexible and they had to be prepared to follow the money.

Raoul Moat was still at secondary school whilst the social and economic landscape was changing but it would directly shape his future prospects. Whilst his brother Angus concentrated on his studies, Raoul did not consider that college was for him. He still loved the outdoors and enjoyed fishing, and he was less inclined to stay at home with books. Without doubt, the occasions when he felt happiest were when he spent time in the countryside, which, for him, meant Rothbury.

This town sits only about thirty miles north of Newcastle but is strikingly different. It is a small market town sheltered in the Northumbrian countryside, surrounded by farmland and is bordered at its southern end by the pretty river Coquet. Like a lot of small rural towns, life there appears unchanging and timeless but naturally over the course of time it has been subject to change and even misery as it frequently suffered bloody raids made by clans along the Scottish borders. At the height of its fortunes the town had a railway and a cinema but these eventually closed and the 'village', as most residents still think of it, returned to a quieter pace of life.

It was a mode of living that Raoul Moat loved and he talked frequently about his hope one day to settle in Rothbury and even to run his own farm. To Moat, Rothbury meant leaving behind life on the fringes of a city and the chance to forget any difficulty, other than trying to coax fish onto his line.

That year the summer holidays were a respite and once Rothbury was left behind, Moat found that his life was changing once more. His mother had begun a new relationship with a man called Brian Healey and the couple would marry in 1986. Both of Josephine's sons attended, and the photographs show a somewhat self-conscious thirteen-year-old Raoul standing between his mother and brother.

Creating a new family unit always has its complications. It is not easy for anyone to step into the role of step parent and clashes about authority and about each member's role in the expanded family can create points of friction. Phrases such as, 'You can't tell me what to do, you are not my father' are commonplace as children struggle to recognise that a parental role has been filled, even if this 'replacement parent' was something they had initially desired.

Raoul and Angus were still close; they would enjoy each other's company on holidays, typically spent in a caravan in the countryside. Raoul had asthma but this did not stop him from indulging in his pastimes, which included fishing. Whilst Angus would stay on at school and study for his A levels, Raoul was less sure about his future. As time went on, the teenage Raoul would fall out with his stepfather, they would clash, and Angus remembers that there were angry exchanges. Yet on the whole the older Moat boy's relationship with Brian was cordial and he has spoken of him as a decent man.

In time Raoul found a new interest: karate. This helped him with his transition from leaving school and entering the adult world, and gave him a focus. This martial art lays emphasis on discipline and restraint – all children who join classes are told in no uncertain terms that karate is a system of self-defence, and it is not a platform for aggression or violence. It was a form of self-discipline that appealed to Raoul, as he was, after all, in control of how he could teach his body and mind to learn new skills – even if he had little control either over his home environment or his work prospects.

His mother remembers this as a time when Raoul began to physically alter. He lost a lot of weight but no doubt gained a leaner and more defined physique. He was tired, she thought, but that is perhaps not surprising, as he was growing quickly and would eventually grow to be six inches taller than his older brother.

She also remembered other aspects about his appearance changed too: he grew his hair longer and beaded it. That in itself represents nothing remarkable – part and parcel of reaching adolescence is creating a new identity, separate and distinct from the parental figures, and a presence that is demonstrated by way of an outward display of difference. It does not mean that the teenager is 'troubled', or at least is as likely to be bothered by nothing more than the issues that all teens face. Studies have also shown that such young adults are more likely to be risk takers, as they have not formed the cognitive ability to understand the consequences of their actions. It is a time when peer attitudes matter more than those of a parent, and so attempts to impress friends can lead to excessive drinking and dangerous pranks.

It is a crucial time in creating a new identity but forming a positive self-image can be difficult. Now that Angus was studying for his degree, Raoul had to consider his place in the world. Karate helped – he proved adept and diligent student – but that would not provide him with an income and the opportunity to gain his independence. He needed a job.

In the end, he found work as a panel beater. He'd been on a number of training courses since leaving school at sixteen and working with his hands suited Raoul. Panel beating, reshaping and remodelling the body panels of cars, would also feed into a new enjoyment that would become an abiding interest – renovating, or 'doing up', cars.

By the time he was 19, a lot had changed for Raoul. His interest in karate had led him into weightlifting and body building. He started to gain body mass and the image of a slight boy with a weak chest and red hair was fast receding. He also noted that the more muscular he became the more female attention he gained.

Powerful male physiques have long held a place in the notion of the ideal male form. Think of classical sculptures like Michelangelo's David, a statue that is five hundred years old but not dissimilar to the photos of physiques that appear in men's health magazines today. But rather than have a consistent appeal, the 'ideal' male form is subject to fashion and socio-economic factors too. Women's figures in fashion spreads are commonly fuller in figure in times of economic hardship, yet when times are good, they shrink to a more androgynous form.

Fashion seems to reflect a desire to see traditional and robust figures when times are hard and that trend is apparent in male fashion too. The tougher the climate, the more we respond to physiques that suggest that a man can 'take care of himself'. Those who book male models have noted that there is a resurgence of the demand for powerfully built males, last seen during the recession in the early 1990s and then directly after the attacks of 9/11.

While the last UK recession was at its worst, Raoul was living out the remaining two years of his teens. The area was once more about to feel the impact of economic downturn. During the 1980s, the North East had struggled. Alongside Liverpool, Manchester, Sheffield, Leeds and Birmingham,

Newcastle-upon-Tyne was one of the cities that was hit hardest by falling employment. By the time of the recession in the early 1990s, it was Liverpool and Newcastle that experienced the deepest recession in terms of employment prospects, with one in five out of work. If you lost your job in the 1980s slump, the average claimant period was nine years. Essentially, these cities had not recovered from the 1980s recession before the 1990s downturn hit.

It was not an easy time to be a young man finding his way in the world but Raoul was coping. His body building had become central to his identity and although he enjoyed being able to project himself as a powerful man, this macho posing had its darker side.

The time that Raoul began 'working out' coincided with an increased misuse of anabolic steroids throughout the world of body building. The steroids are a synthetically-manufactured variant of the group of hormones which occur naturally in the body, and have a mass-producing effect on the physique and increase muscle tissue. Athletes began to use them as early as the 1950s and by the 1970s they were banned by the International Olympic Committee. However, that didn't stop their use and misuse and by the 1980s there were a number of 'doping scandals' and several famous athletes failed tests and were banned from competing.

It was only a matter of time before these drugs became

available in private gyms and were seen as a quick way to acquire body mass. Some surveys estimate that 20 per cent of those attending gyms for body building have used anabolic steroids; other surveys suggest that the figure could be as high as 40 per cent. The north-east of England is thought to be the region that has the highest lifetime use of steroids.

It is significant that people who have misused steroids do not think of themselves as drug abusers – many seem unaware that using these substances is illegal – and instead see themselves as 'self improvers'. They take care of their bodies by other common measures, such as the use of vitamins and maintaining a controlled diet. Anabolic steroids, in fact, seem to feed into the idea that the user is taking control and making active choices about their bodies, and so the idea of inflicting damage to their health hardly concurs with the image such folk hold of themselves as self-determining.

Experts do not agree unanimously that anabolic steroids, intensive training, and a high protein diet builds body weight and muscles but, on balance, this probably is the case. Once users can see a rapid development, many come to endorse, and then rely on, the drug. There is also some dispute about possible side effects. Some users find they feel more aggressive, competitive and better able to perform strenuous physical activity and again, these characteristics then add to the drug's appeal. But some heavy users are said to have experienced 'roid rage' – fits of physical and even sexual violence. Yet there are those who argue that users who develop roid rage were already prone to violent tendencies.

Other side effects include liver abnormalities, hypertension and changes to the male reproductive system. Sperm output and quality is reduced, and although sex drive may at first increase, it can then be lowered. Anabolic steroids can be taken orally but can also be administered in liquid form via injection, something that carries a far higher risk both in terms of managing doses and other considerations, such as contracting HIV and other infections associated with shared needle use.

But these things rarely enter the thoughts of a user. One former advocate of steroids spoke anonymously about the attraction of the drug. He pointed out that they are in demand because they work, and that for bodybuilders, getting bigger is the overriding goal. He saw widespread misuse across a number of disciplines however, and not just body building – rugby and marital arts enthusiasts also indulged.

This character did not experience the 'roid rage' he noticed in others, but was of the opinion that these types were volatile before they became users. Yet for some, steroids were not the only drugs being misused and he offered this insight: 'An interesting point to note when looking at people suffering from roid rage is that many users also indulge in other recreational drug use, such as cocaine and ephedrine.'

He continued: 'These drugs are known to increase aggression in some users. Combine that with a raised level of testosterone and you could well be lighting the blue touch paper.'

The blue touch paper would become an issue in the life of Raoul Moat. He was getting plenty of female attention now; he was getting work here and there and found that he could supplement his income by working as a 'door security man' in the evenings. He had moved a long way from the unhappiness and insecurities of his childhood, something Angus has described as 'a troublesome and traumatic time'.

Yet although Raoul was physically transformed, how far a journey had his mind taken him from his formative experiences? The former steroid user referred to above may not have known Raoul Moat, but he encountered many who were similar to the man now bulked up beyond recognition. 'What I will say,' he remarked, 'is that if you are happy with who you are then there is no place for steroids in your life. Most users are reaching for something they haven't got.'

CHAPTER SEVEN
ESCALATION
SUNDAY 4 JULY

They've hunted me for years, now its my turn.
– from Raoul Moat's letters

Moat had been doing a lot of thinking. Now that his adrenalin had subsided, and his name and his picture had been broadcast across the TV and taken up column inches in newspapers, he was not happy with the way his actions were portrayed as a 'grudge'. Moat did not like to be misunderstood. His friends knew that and he decided to call on one of them that night.

Andy McAllister was watching TV at his home in Kenton late on Saturday night when he heard a knock on the door. He had known Moat previously, but he was the last person McAllister expected to hear from, given the drama he, along with the rest of the British public, had seen unfolding on the news. He was about to get the shock of his life. When the dad-of-five opened the door he saw Moat standing outside, waiting to talk to him. McAllister could not quite believe his eyes, for he had been following the story of the murder of Chris Brown and the shooting of Sam Stobbart all day. Moat wanted to come in.

Raoul was wearing jeans, a cream coloured tee shirt and a military style hat, and was very calm, saying that he wanted to explain his side of the story before things were twisted any further. He said that in the early hours he had sat under the window and had to listen as the group inside talked about him and laughed. He'd grown angrier as the minutes passed and then he had snapped, unable to take anymore.

McAllister listened as he talked and it struck him how measured Moat was. His visitor did not raise his voice or remonstrate, there was an eerie distance as he recounted all that he had done. McAllister was blunt. He told Moat that he should hand himself in and that he would accompany him to the station if that would help. But the gunman said: 'No I've got nothing left Andy – and I fully intend to take as many police as I can with me.'

It was a chilling turn in Moat's thinking. He asked McAllister for a mobile phone to allow him to speak to the police, and shortly after midnight he walked back out into the night.

David Rathband didn't grow up on Tyneside, he is originally from Stafford but he was proud to serve the Northumbria police force and had done so for the last 10 years. Married with two children, he enjoyed his work although he realised it had its risks and exposed you to some of the worst aspects of human nature.

He knew about the events of the previous evening at Birtley and was stationed at the roundabout where the A1 meets the A69 in his marked police car, a Volvo, when he decided to send a text to his wife Kath. He knew the roundabout well and often chose that particular spot to wait at, since it was the place where arterial roads in and out of the city met, and provided an ideal vantage point to view any traffic incidents which might be taking place.

PC Rathband had been parked there for over an hour watching traffic, observing all the usual comings and goings of an early Sunday morning, as revellers from Saturday night made their way home, and he thought it was relatively quiet given that it was a summer's evening. Rathband knew that Moat was on the run and, by then, all units were aware of the registration details of the car that they suspected Moat might be using. On-board computers meant that with automatic numberplate recognition, PC Rathband would be alerted should Moat drive by. He thought that it was a possibility, as the roundabout stands close to Birtley and near to where Moat would try to escape from the city, down the M6 for example, assuming he was planning to go to ground.

In reality, experience had taught Rathband that the chances of spotting Raoul Moat were slim. Police work is very often about patience and endeavour, but surveillance work, where the suspect has not been pinned to an exact location, is often fruitless. It was all about luck. Not that he was wasting his time. Moat was one offender, but there were any number of other crimes being committed in the city that night that would also need detecting.

It was coming up to quarter-to-one in the morning and he and his wife had finished texting each other about their daughter's birthday party. Kath Rahband knew about Moat's rampage too and asked her husband to be careful. She'd been clearing out a cupboard at home and they'd joked with one another that that would be a good place to hide from any gunman. As he placed his phone in the car's door compartment, the policeman had a feeling that someone was watching him.

As he looked up, he saw a man jogging over to his car from only a few feet away. He reasoned that the jogger must have emerged from behind one of the concrete pillars and realised that it was Raoul Moat. It was only when he was approaching the car that Rathband saw that Moat had something in his hands. The officer started to process this rush of information. The oncoming man was holding the stock of the shotgun with his right hand, its barrel with his left.

He saw the man slow as he reached the car. The gunman

was facing the passenger side window and he raised his weapon. All this action concertinaed into seconds, and PC Rathband was aware that his life was in danger. Moat fired the gun between the officer's eyes. PC Rathband felt his face explode. The noise was deafening and of such intensity that the victim believed it was the noise alone that was causing him such excruciating pain.

The shotgun had discharged 200 pieces of shot directly into his face and PC Rathband experienced unbearable pain from the top of his head to his throat. He sensed straightaway that his right eye had been irreparably damaged by the discharge — it was almost as if it had been sucked out by the force of the blast. And he knew instinctively that he would never see from it again.

Rathband had been thrown into the foot-well of the car but he still had his seatbelt on and he began to try to remove it. He knew that he must summon help, but was also aware that the inside of the patrol car was illuminated. That meant that Moat could see what he had done but would also be witness to Rathband's frantic efforts to raise the alarm.

The injured man sat up and started to fumble for the button on his car's screen that would relay an emergency message: it would also activate the car, making the cab 'live', allowing Rathband to communicate with his colleagues, who would be able to hear what was happening. It was at this point that Rathband realised that his attacker was still

RAOUL MOAT

there, watching him. The blinded man could not see and he could not find the emergency button. Moat raised the gun again.

Instinct took over, as Rathband raised his left hand to his face. He had pivoted slightly in his seat and that meant that the second shot entered his shoulder. The police officer knew then that Moat was intent on killing him. He slumped to the side in an effort to play dead. He was aware that he could hear strange noises and then realised that it was the result of blood and air evacuating from the injures in his face. He made a huge effort to hold his breath and try to remain motionless.

Moat then walked away but Rathband remained still. He was fortunate that he had managed to grasp the police radio and had to wait in frustration as he heard another colleague relay a message before he could raise the alarm – the radio permits only one transmission at a time. Eventually he was able to pick up the carrier signal and he broadcast that he needed urgent assistance as he'd been shot. He listened to the radio traffic and he heard a voice he knew asking, 'Can you GPS David?' All cars can be located via GPS but the system can be slow. That urged Rathband on, he felt that he could summon the strength to radio in his exact location. He pushed open his door and heard sirens approaching. He also knew that if he could hear them, Moat could too.

Moments earlier, a taxi driver drove onto the roundabout

heading from the A69. He had heard the shot through his open window and saw a man jogging away from a police patrol car and towards a black car parked on the slip road.

The car drove off and the taxi driver rushed to the patrol car – he could see the police officer had been badly wounded but as he did not have any medical training he knew that he was not in a position to help. He wasn't even sure if the policeman was alive but saw an ambulance and gave chase: he knew he had to stop it and so flashed his lights and blasted his horn until it pulled over.

By the time the taxi driver returned to the roundabout, the ambulance having raced ahead of him, the scene had been transformed. PC Rathband's radio alert meant that a number of armed police and response cars had arrived. A gunman was on the loose but the first concern had to be for David Rathband; there were two hundred shotgun pellets in his skull and as he was being treated at the roadside by paramedics, the fear was that the gunshot had caused severe and lasting damage. Rathband was not sure if he would survive and asked the medic treating him to tell his wife and children that he loved them.

He was taken to Newcastle General Hospital and that left a number of personnel still gathered at the roundabout. One thought was on everyone's mind. If Moat was responsible for this attack, then that meant that the murder enquiry had taken on a new and worrying dimension: Moat was targeting police officers.

Those leading the enquiry would learn later that the news that a fellow officer had been shot came in only approximately 10 minutes after Moat had put down the phone, after concluding a call to other officers. Moat had spoken for around six minutes, outlining his grievances against the police. It was not the only call he was to make that night. At 1.35am, he dialled 999 again and complained that the police were not taking him seriously enough.

But Moat was wrong. Northumbria Police was taking Raoul Thomas Moat very seriously indeed.

The police were under pressure to release information about the case and a statement was issued. It read:

> A Northumbria Police Officer has been seriously injured after being attacked by an armed man described as dangerous.
>
> At 12.45am today (Sunday, July 4) police received reports of an incident on the Western Bypass at East Denton, Newcastle.
>
> A uniformed motor patrols officer was carrying out static patrol on the roundabout which adjoins the A1 and the A69.
>
> He was approached by a man who was armed. The officer suffered a gunshot wound and was taken to Newcastle General Hospital where his condition is

described as serious but not thought to be life-threatening at this time.

Police strongly believe that this shooting is linked to the incident in Gateshead in the early hours of Saturday morning, during which a man was killed and a woman seriously injured.

We are currently following up several lines of enquiry. All available police resources and tactics are being used.

Temporary Chief Constable Sue Sim said: 'This was an unprovoked attack on a Northumbria Police officer as he carried out his duty. My thoughts are with his family and colleagues at this time.

'We strongly believe that this was carried out by the same man who shot two people in Gateshead early yesterday morning.

'Raoul Thomas Moat is a wanted man. He is very dangerous and should not be approached by members of the public.

'We know that Moat held a grudge against the people he targeted in Gateshead yesterday. It is now believed his grudge at the moment is with the police.'

It was clear that the calls allowed Raoul Moat to air his grievances but that was not where his attempt to justify his actions ended. Far from it. Moat sat down and wrote a letter and then he decided to deliver it to Andy McAllister's house in person. It seemed an extraordinary thing to do. As he approached PC Rathband's patrol car and took the conscious decision to shoot the officer, Moat's system would have been flooded with adrenalin. It is almost impossible to imagine how he could find paper and a pen, and then sit down to start writing out his thoughts. The letter would amount to 49 pages – there are few mistakes and the handwriting is legible. This was not a briefly dashed off note and in it, Moat sets out a good deal about the way he viewed his situation and gives an invaluable insight into how his mind worked. *The Sun* newspaper exclusively published the letter:

On the night 3/7/10 I shot Chris Brown and Samantha Stobbart, after an argument earlier that evening, and here I will make all the facts clear so there is no missunderstanding about the events which took place and, the build up to these events…

Hid under Jackie's window and waited. For an hour and a half, I listened to them mocking me.

It was hurtful listening to Sam, especially after nearly six years. They had opened a window and I could hear everything.

If I was ever going to back down, listening to them stopped that.

At 2.30am, they came out. I shot him in the chest

and he ran off. Sam screamed and tried to stop me as I gave chase.

I fired the second and he went down. I pointed the gun at Sam to chase her and she ran off.

I reloaded two customised rounds. Sam's was half the powder, with small-gauge pellets. With a superficial injury she would get massive compensation payout for her, inadvertently providing for me when I'm gone.

And there would be small scarring, reminding her not to ever do this to anyone again. How could she have done this to me? I put the third round into his head and went to the window and fired at Sam. It hit but she seemed OK but I paused to be sure. She crawled to the kitchen quickly and hid behind the door.

I looked around for anyone else to shoot, there was no one, looked back at Sam, went to shoot myself, then changed my mind.

It's like the Hulk, it takes over and it's more than anger and it happens only when I'm hurt, and this time I was really hurt.

I've slept one hour per night for weeks now. It feels like I'm watching a film, not real at all.

Moat wanted it made known that he felt provoked by Sam. He wrote long passages in the letter about how much she had meant to him, that Sam fulfilled him as no other woman had. In his mind then, the 'fall' Sam took was from a very considerable height. Here was a woman he imagined would make him whole and yet she betrayed him when he felt that he needed her support most – when he was 'taking a stand' and going to prison to prove that he was willing to fight for the truth as he saw it.

The police receive a good deal of attention in the letters too, for what Moat saw as their persecution of him. He wrote:

> Looking at my arrests you can draw only one conclusion, but again 90% is rubbish, with many being stitch ups. Most of what I've done I've gotten away with, no arrest. I can now say that I've been a bad lad, but the arrests are the untrue side of that, and is mostly the police being witch hunters…The crimes I have committed are to people who have wronged me in some way.

For Moat, this helped underpin his conviction that he had been poorly treated by the police but there was a more vehement statement to follow. He continued:

> Last night I called 999 and declared war on Northumbria Police before shooting an officer on the West End A69 roundabout in his T5. Sitting there waiting to bully someone.

> Probably a single mum who couldn't afford her
> car tax.
> Rang again and told them they're gonna pay for
> what they've done to me and Sam. I went straight
> but they couldn't let it go.
> The public need not fear me but the police should as
> I won't stop till I'm dead.

This is an attempt to shift blame and muddy the waters as to why he acted as he did. He shot a defenceless officer but in his mind, the police had brought retribution on themselves. He did not act out of fury for himself he stresses, but he was championing the defenceless, the lone mums who'd been singled out because they can't afford car tax. Yet there was another single mother in his thoughts of course, one he had shot 24 hours earlier and he does feel remorse, yet even this is couched in threat. He writes:

> Those doctors better save her or I'll hit that
> hospital. I still love her despite everything but my
> head is a mess right now and I know I'm too far
> gone to make much sense of it.
> I guess I've finally lost it. I'm not on the run, I will
> keep killing police until I am dead.
> They've hunted me for years, now it's my turn.
> I am very sorry about Sam and wish I hadn't shot
> at her. Just make sure she stays alive.

> I never cheated on her, I wish she hadn't on me.
> She pulled the trigger by doing so just as much as me.

The police were in no doubt now that they were dealing with a man who felt he had lost everything and was willing and able to act on his violent threats. By 6am Northumbria Police told the press that the shootings of PC Rathband, Samantha Stobbart and Chris Brown were linked and Raoul Moat was a 'wanted man'.

By that afternoon, they knew a great deal more about Moat and a strategy not only of how to capture him but how best to communicate to him was being devised. At 2pm, the police made a direct appeal to Moat and urged him to hand himself in for the sake of his three children. One of them, Chanel, his youngest, had a mother in hospital who had been seriously wounded by her father.

Sam was in surgery for five hours as the team fought to stabilise her condition, examine the extent of her injuries and begin repairs. She had serious internal injuries and if her arm had absorbed some of the shot's impact, the blast's full force could have killed her.

The appeal did not result in Moat handing himself in. He was now the focus of a growing manhunt but, of course, Raoul had written that he was not on the run. He was at war but was not hiding from them, and he was prepared to die. He was a mission killer.

Organising a 'hunt' in such circumstances is a fraught affair.

Officers were targets, even following standard procedures and making house-to-house enquires could now expose them as 'soft targets'. The enquiry into his whereabouts held considerable risks. Moat could be anywhere. Or nowhere.

CHAPTER EIGHT
1998

A lot had changed in the previous few years and for Moat, these changes were both good and bad. He had left home and reached an understanding with himself that he no longer wanted to stay in contact with his mother.

The last time that he saw her he had barely said a word; he didn't know where to begin. Since his grandmother had died two years earlier, he'd seen less of Angus too. Their lives were different in so many ways now that perhaps a lack of communication was inevitable. Angus had done well: after graduating, he'd gone on to study for his masters and he looked set to succeed. He wouldn't just have a job, he'd have a career.

That kind of life was a world away from the one that Raoul now inhabited but in truth, this other set of circumstances were ones that he was managing well. He weighed almost 18 stone and, at 25 years old, he was at his physical peak. He had friends now, a group of men who understood the rules of advancement of life on the streets, the grey economy where cash traded hands, goods, both legal and illegal, were moved along the chain of supply and demand and territory was fought for.

Raoul Moat did not see himself as a criminal, although he knew those who were. He was a different breed. Self-sufficient, able to dip in and out of illicit activities, a man who knew how to take care of himself: nobody's fool but not a major player, and not someone who would work his way through the ranks of a serious and organised criminal gang.

Moat knew that you have to be a big man on the street if you expect not to get messed with: no one is on-hand to sort out trouble for you, certainly not the police. In a dog-eat-dog world, the young man found that he was doing okay, in part because he had the muscle to back himself and also because he was intelligent. He knew who to rely on, who had to be kept in line and who would be useful to him in the long run. And when it came down to it, he didn't shy away from violence. In his world, your size meant nothing if all the threat and dominance that such macho display implied wasn't backed up by a show of force. Once you opened your mouth and made a threat, you were obliged to act on it. If you didn't, you were finished, a laughing stock.

The problem with this way of life is that it is one of diminishing returns. At its best, cash is flowing, girls are plentiful, there were plenty of laughs to be had and you are certain of your place somewhere near the top of the pecking order. But at its worst, Moat was smart enough to know that the walls of the existence he had constructed were constantly closing in. There was always a threat from somewhere, someone younger coming up, the wrong word said to the wrong man, the police, and the complications that inevitably arose when relationships turned sour. He sensed that it was an empire built on sand and that the sands were always shifting. He took illegal drugs such as ecstasy or amphetamines when he needed to, either to anaesthetise him to his condition or simply to have a laugh with his friends; sometimes he just needed the distraction. Interestingly, he didn't drink. His drug-taking, like everything else in his life now, was on his terms. He didn't like what he saw when people drank – to him they looked like idiots.

The embryo hard man liked having his own place. He had a one-bedroom flat and he indulged in his love of animals. He kept dogs, huskies and later pit bulls, but perhaps reptiles were his most treasured possessions. Over the years, he kept all sorts: lizards, terrapins, an albino python and a boa constrictor. Keeping snakes isn't straightforward – it is a lot more involved than just buying a glass tank and hoping for the best. They have to be kept at a constant temperature, with heat lamps used to provide a steady warmth of above 28 degrees plus a 'basking spot' of about 32 degrees and a 'hide' should be provided for the snakes to shelter in. And of course there's the diet to consider. Younger snakes are fed mice and, as they reach maturity, they consume rats or rabbits. This kind of 'meat' can be purchased and kept in a deep freeze and then thawed out come feeding time.

Moat found that, on the whole, women weren't too keen on his snakes – they are hardly cuddly or responsive, but he liked them. Raoul liked to watch them and handle them, and the larger the boa constrictor grew, the more impressive it was. It grew to ten feet in length, it was heavy, and none of his girlfriends felt comfortable handling it. He found it fascinating to feel its coils of pure muscle as it glided over skin, edging and positioning itself around your neck and torso. A snake is indifferent to its prey; all it focuses on is the efficacy of a kill. It doesn't strike, it waits and moves with an exactitude, knowing how much power to exercise as it squeezes the life from its quarry. The more the prey struggles, the easier the constrictor finds it to pull its coils tighter. This snake has infinite patience. Moat admired that.

As mentioned before, he also kept dogs, huskies and pit

bull terriers. It doesn't take a degree in psychology to guess that the man was attracted to exotic pets and powerful dogs because he felt that they reflected his self-image — namely that they were dangerous if not handled correctly. One friend recalls a pit bull so savage that Moat had to keep the canine chained to a wall unless he was there to handle it, and it is doubtful that the Dangerous Dogs Act troubled him too greatly. The Act was first introduced in 1991 after a spate of attacks by dogs on children and it focused on regulating the ownership of pit bull terriers, Japanese Tosas, the Fila Brasileiros and the Dogo Argentinos plus any crossbreeds of the four varieties. But in fact, any dog found to be 'dangerously out of control in a public place' can be destroyed and the owner fined or imprisoned.

The act was unpopular amongst many of the owners of the breeds in question and the RSPCA did not think it helpful that certain types of dogs were 'demonised'. How a dog behaves, of course, relies on how it is trained and kept, but what is troubling is that historically, pit bulls were bred to show aggression — towards other dogs — and to fight to the death. In the wrong hands, such animals can be used as macho props. At their worst, 'weapon dogs' have been used by criminals to cause injury and as a way of protecting their assets. In fact, the dogs can be used in much the same way as a criminal might wield a knife or a gun. Again, these associations will attract certain men, men who are concerned about how they are perceived and their status on the streets.

Moat knew a great deal about how he came across to others and about how aggression could be used to stamp his authority. This was about more than 'working the doors', where it was essential to be seen as a man not to be messed with. Needless to say, even though he stood at six-foot three-inches and was muscle-bound, that did not stop the occasional drunk from chancing his arm, and such characters soon found that Moat didn't hesitate to use his bulk. And of course, it wasn't just men who were aware of Moat's physicality – women were too.

By now, Moat was used to getting his share of female attention; certain women admired his size and were attracted to the fact that as a doorman, he could show them special favours. On a night out, standing outside in long queues waiting to get inside a club can be tedious and can ruin the buzz of a good time and so learning to charm your way into an entry ahead of others can be part and parcel of a great evening. Doormen know that women try and flirt as a way of getting preferential treatment and the favours don't have to stop there. There can be free drinks if the doorman gives the nod and access to so-called 'VIP' areas – parts of the club that are sectioned off for exclusive use of minor celebrities or, in recent times, the 'major celebrity' that comes with being a Premiership footballer.

Football has a particular place in the hearts of most

residents of Newcastle and despite the fact that the 'Magpies' club hasn't won any silverware for over 35 years, it still enjoys huge support and a loyal following. But football has long since stopped being wholly confined to what happens on the pitch and it can be argued that when the Spice Girls' Victoria Adams began dating Manchester United footballer David Beckham in 1997, football began to feature as much in the front pages of the tabloids as it had dominated the back ones. As wages began to spiral into tens of thousands of pounds per week for stars of the Premiership, football became the profession that more and more young boys began to aspire to. Gone were the ideas of becoming a fireman or a train driver – being a footballer now meant undreamed of wealth and status, as well as the prospect of spending time at one long and uninterrupted PE lesson.

Young girls too started to look to the future with different expectations, and the idea that being a 'glamour model' was a profession, and to some a more attractive one than being a teacher or a nurse could ever be, began to take hold. When 'Posh Spice' teamed up with 'Becks', it seemed that the whole of the country developed a new and seemingly insatiable interest in the love lives of 'celebs' and in February 1999, a new magazine called *Heat* was launched to serve just that interest.

Moat had witnessed some of the fringes of this world, letting footballers into the club and being on nodding terms with some of them. He also saw how girls responded to them and in a minor way, how they responded to him and his influence at the club. Why not milk it? He was a young man in his prime and although he might not ever pull down the kind of salary that attracted some of the women in the club, he wasn't short of attention either. Women drifted in and out of his life; some were no more than one night stands, while some hung around for a little longer; and, if some reports are to be believed, Moat became a father.

Whether this is true or not cannot be ascertained; there is some suggestion that he may have fathered as many as six children and that he lost touch with three of them as the years passed. Again, this may be little more than speculation but if it is true, the notion of fatherhood will not have been an easy one for Moat to have coped with. With no interaction with his own biological father and with a difficult relationship with the man that later became his stepfather, Raoul had little actual experience of how it felt to be fathered. He had his own ideas and he had begun a relationship with a woman that would change his life. He had met Marissa Reid.

Marissa was young, only 19 years old, when she was introduced to Moat on a blind date and was impressed by him. She would later say: 'What woman wouldn't find Raoul attractive; he did have a muscular physique.' At the outset of the relationship, she said that Moat seemed a caring, gentle and a loving person. He was considerate and the perfect gentleman and that had been evident on the night that they met as he ended the evening with a very chaste kiss on the cheek. As the months passed however, Marissa said that she then began to see a different side to Raoul. He became possessive, jealous and angry if he felt that she had behaved in a way that he did not like and started to physically abuse her.

This would fit the profile of a typical male domestic abuser and the pattern of behaviour is well documented. Abusers can be caring and demonstrative about their feelings of affection, a so-called 'honeymoon' period, but behind the declaration of love lies a desire to dominate and control the object of their affection. Any dissent or deviation from their expectations as to how a partner should behave can result in an outburst that includes more than the use of violence.

Women who have remained trapped in relationships with abusers have spoken of a number of different strategies employed against them. The abuser belittles them, insults and undermines their self-confidence, for example attacking how they look and stating that no other man would put up with them. Or they become isolated from friends and family as the abuser demands that they spend time with him exclusively, using jealousy as an excuse. Smashing things and losing all control when 'pushed' is another aspect, again demonstrating that they have no control over their emotions when 'wound up'. This at once can intimidate and underlines the fact that the abuser is not to blame, that their outburst has been provoked.

Another tactic is to threaten to self-harm. Men have been known to smash their hands through window panes, throw themselves down a flight of stairs and say that they will commit suicide if a partner does not forgive them or continue the relationship. Moat is said to have been hospitalised after an overdose of the drug GHB after a break up with a girlfriend and received a psychiatric assessment.

Children are also used as a weapon; the threat can be made that they will be taken away or that social services will be called and that the partner will be deemed an unfit mother. The range of threat and mind games used is as many and varied as there are dysfunctional relationships, and yet what links them is the desire of the abuser to control a partner's actions.

These relationships can continue for years and for those who have never understood the dynamic, it can be difficult to understand why women don't break away. There is also the misconception that women 'choose' violent men but research highlighted by Women's Aid shows that for 51 per cent of the women surveyed, the first incidence of domestic violence occurred after one year or more; for 30 per cent of the sample it happened between three months and a year. For 13 per cent, violence was initiated between one and three months, whereas for six per cent abuse occurred within less than a month. So for the majority of women, the relationship had begun on a different footing and was well established before the first incident of violence occurred; making many women believe that either it will not happen again or that their partners will not resort to abuse if they 'change' their own behaviour and appease their partner.

If the cycle of abuse continues, the question is raised as to why women simply don't just walk away. Economic realities certainly have a part to play and Shelter have reported that 40 per cent of the women they dealt with counted domestic violence as a factor in their homelessness and, of course, not all women are able to face life on the streets to escape an attacker at home. And in fact, even if a woman flees from the house she shared with an abuser, it will not be enough to guarantee her safety. As has been stated earlier, it is often the case that women are most vulnerable to attack once they leave their home.

Marissa Reid has told the press that she was physically abused by Moat and described one incident where a baseball bat was held to her throat until she broke free, that she was then hit in the back with the bat by Moat and that he held her by the neck until she passed out.

A friend loyal to Moat denied that the relationship was as violent as Marissa has portrayed it, and yet he did think Moat was capable of lashing out. He thought the relationship was far from perfect but also saw blame on both sides, and perceived a degree of unhappiness that they both shared. It might sound evasive or blinkered, but Marissa knew something more about how desperate and irrational Moat's state of mind could be. A year into the relationship, they shared a bizarre suicide pact.

Marissa had found out that Moat had been seeing an ex-girlfriend and she became very upset. Moat then gave her a choice that will have surprised those who worked with him. She said: 'He told me he couldn't choose between us and the only way we could stay together was if we killed ourselves. I was besotted with Raoul. I couldn't get him out of my head. He controlled me totally and utterly. I was so scared of him I'd do anything and everything he asked.'

The couple travelled to a local beauty spot and Marissa says that they took an overdose of Nytol and vodka and Moat told her that he was afraid to die alone. They both lost consciousness but when Marissa came round, she panicked and ran to a police officer she saw walking by and told him what had happened. They both received treatment and Marissa believed that Moat's enlarged heart, a result of steroid abuse, allowed him to survive the suicide attempt. She was then horrified to learn that Moat had decided to see his ex rather than her. Fairly soon, however, they were back together and it is easy to see that the joint suicide pact could be seen as a dramatic attempt to control her.

Three years later, at the age of 23, Marissa gave birth to the first of two daughters she would have with Moat. She claimed that during her second pregnancy, Moat left her for another young woman and she believes that he was repeatedly unfaithful but that he would almost certainly have killed her if he believed that she was having an affair herself.

During one outburst when he believed that she had been flirting with another man at a club, Marissa claims that Moat tied her to their bed and raped her. She said: 'That man was a living, breathing monster.' The man that had spoken with Marissa is said to have been taken outside the club and beaten by Moat.

Marital rape is another typical feature in domestic abuse cases and the refusal of a female partner to agree to sex is a trigger point for abusers. Again, they seek to assert their control over a partner they see as defiant. Sexual jealousy also has a part to play in defining the actions of an abuser, as their fears about their own deeply hidden inadequacy leaves them to suspect that they will be usurped by another man. It is a toxic mix of need and fear in themselves that abusers cannot admit to. They may confess to remorse after a violent outburst but hidden in that supposed guilt is the impulse to blame others – typified by sentiments such as: *You pushed me, it is only because I feel about you so strongly.*

In addition, no amount of sorrow after the event appears to prevent the abuser from repeating his actions. It is a very difficult pattern to break and psychologist Professor Craig Jackson has said: 'The best predictor of future behaviour is past behaviour.' The abuser will have learned over many years that intimidation and violence are effective ways to impose his will. It should not be forgotten that, for the abuser, feelings of frustration, upset and anxiety are real; but if that man has not learned how to cope with distress, the result can be catastrophic.

The returns on violent and abusive behaviour also become reduced over time. They may mean that an abuser remains nominally in control of a relationship but resentment and fear accumulates and prevents a partnership from functioning in a healthy way. Intimacy becomes impossible as trust is unattainable and the cycle of fear and anxiety on both sides of the divide multiply. Children that grow up in an abusive household are not immune from what they observe even if they are not directly targeted by an abuser. Although all children respond differently, emotional and behavioural problem, as well as feelings of shame and guilt, are common.

Once children are introduced into an abusive relationship the stakes are inevitably higher as dependency at once deepens a mother's vulnerability and heightens an abusive father's sense of entitlement and a need to assert his control over the household. One girl who grew up with an abusive stepfather from the age of seven described her early life as part of a testimonial on a website. She wrote: 'It didn't take long for me to realise how violent The Monster was. I lived in fear constantly. He rarely hit anyone; he didn't have to. The threats, coupled with the verbal and emotional abuse, were more than enough to keep us all under his control. Occasionally, he would slap me or my mother to punctuate a point. He was a master of psychological manipulation. He loved to play games.'

The ability to manipulate is another common thread in the psychological makeup of an abuser. Very often, few outside the family are aware that abuse is an issue. Friends talk in glowing terms about the abuser's qualities – they are capable of presenting an image of amiability and this is perhaps not so much of a sham as a genuine desire to hold their own in the status of male friendship groups. When crossed however, the same friends will admit that the abuser 'knew how to stand his ground', 'would not be walked over', and when it comes to the possibility that the same friend could slap a wife or girlfriend, some admit: 'I'm not saying that he didn't.'

The use of violence is divisive but morally it is a grey area. Boys grow up in a culture that does recognise the legitimacy of violence in certain circumstances, from war movies to the self-sufficiency of characters like Bruce Willis's John McClane in *Die Hard*. The film spawned a number of sequels and when the character was first introduced in 1988, he had separated from his wife and notably it was his ability to evade capture by terrorists and kill them one by one that restores his wife's faith in him.

The same character that has a heavy drinking habit, cannot deal with authority, and is estranged from his family, is the same man audiences cheer on as he wages war against the bad guys. As the trailer announced, 'The last thing McClane wants is to be a hero, but he doesn't have a choice.' His wife Holly knows that McClane is still alive in the building somewhere once she watches one of the terrorists smash a table in frustration, and says: 'Only John can drive somebody that crazy.' What the film illustrated was that McClane's faults became his strengths and it is an aspect of the film that had a strong appeal for its audience.

Despite our protestations that violence is wrong, there is a long tradition of celebrating the man who does take a stand and fights back. As a society, and in fact in all societies stretching back over centuries, we celebrate the 'warrior'. We have fixed ideas of what it means to be 'manly', and it is something that boys have to learn quickly; being a 'mummy's boy' or a 'cry baby' are seen as unattractive traits in boys.

This isn't a system that is laid down by men alone and in fact studies have shown the vital, even if it is an unconscious, role that mothers have in shaping masculine identity. Mothers do not interact with their daughters and their sons in the same way, even from the point of birth. Mothers will look, smile and talk more with their daughters and spend more time communicating with them. When it comes to how they handle their sons, not only do they communicate with them to a lesser degree, they use more severe disciplinary styles and more shaming techniques, and boys are subject to more orders and restrictions.

One experiment even revealed that when mothers were presented with babies wearing gender-neutral clothing, they interpreted a child's expression as one of 'fear' when they were told that the child was a girl and one of 'anger' when they were told the child was a boy. Over a relatively short space of time, boys begin to conduct themselves differently to girls. By the age of four, boys display more aggressive behaviour in play and, interestingly, this cannot be the result of higher levels of testosterone, since the levels of the hormone in boys and girls are comparable until the age of eight.

In truth, we expect our boys to display aggressive traits, we admire and reward them. We place toughness, dominance and the willingness to resort to violence during conflicts at the heart of masculine identity. But knowing when it is 'right' or 'wrong' to use violence is also subject to society's norms, there are standards of behaviour that men are not supposed to transgress. Men are expected to know how to control their aggression. But positive early experiences of how a baby is handled by its primary carer are important, otherwise this can limit a child's ability to develop empathy and impulse control.

Furthermore other studies, particularly ones that focus on why men use violence, have uncovered the fact that masculinity isn't something a man *is*, it is what he *does*. It is active, ongoing and it has been coined as 'doing gender'. One academic, Jessie L. Krienert, summarised it as follows: 'Masculinity must be performed and presented recurrently in any situation – constant self-presentation occurs throughout every social interaction in which a man is involved.'

Marissa Reid has spoken of Moat being 'stressed' when he would return from working on the doors – it was one arena where his masculinity was very visible and at risk of challenge. And it was when he was 'stressed' that he was most likely to lash out at her, unable to separate his role at home from the one that he had to display on the street.

Moat's neighbours may not have known very much about the details of his domestic arrangements but they were clear who Moat was. He was an imposing figure and few would cross him at this time. As the Millennium came and went, it seemed that the city was at long last enjoying a renaissance – the Millennium bridge linking the quayside of Gateshead to that of Newcastle was opened in 2001 and the following year, the flour mill that stood on the banks of Gateshead and that was closed in 1981 was reopened as the

Centre of Contemporary Art. Like a lot of cities, Newcastle showed signs of a new confidence but this self-belief did not spread to all communities and there were pockets once again left behind. Despite the hopes that new Labour would revitalise the north and the introduction of a new raft of initiatives, little changed in areas that had been run-down over the previous three decades. One local news reporter admitted that the sections of the city where Moat resided provided most of the material for crime stories in the entire locality. When looking for comments from local residents, the journalist soon learned to stop asking what people did for a living. Jobs were still scarce and in these islands of deprivation, occupations no longer defined what people did or how they perceived themselves.

Raoul Moat did not see himself as someone who was dependent on state handouts. He wanted to earn for himself and if that meant dipping in and out of criminality, then so be it. It was a resource when other resources were unavailable. And if he had to defend his corner when the time came, then so be it; few people thought that Moat would back down if confronted.

In a study of violent men, Hans Toch uncovered a key insight. He discovered that men like Moat who were not afraid to use violence, and saw the willingness to fight in any given situation as a measure of self-worth, had been subject all their lives to strong feelings of being weak, insignificant, helpless and fearful.

Such contradictions create a volatile and unstable character and the psychohistorian Lloyd deMause succinctly summarises the outlook of such men thus: 'Anything is better than being seen as weak, abandoned, unloved; better to take risks and court death.'

Moat would not have come across this quote but as the first decade of the new millennium dawned, he became a man who understood little else.

CHAPTER NINE
MANHUNT
MONDAY 5 JULY

*I guess I've finally lost it. I'm not on the run,
I will keep killing police until I am dead.*
– from Raoul Moat's letters

It had been a difficult 24 hours. Northumbria police had interviewed Andy MacAllister for a good deal of the previous day, Sunday, as he told them what he could about Moat's visit and the request he had made for a mobile phone. When his statement was finished, MacAllister returned home, only to be woken by a knock on the door in the early hours of Monday morning.

It was Moat with his 'murder statement'. No officers had been conducting a surveillance on the house and so no one was waiting to arrest the killer should he return to see his friend once again. In truth, no one expected the man who had shot three people to return to the same address he'd visited only the night before, but by now it was becoming clear that no one knew Raoul Moat very well at all.

That morning, the police had announced that they were preparing to make another appeal to Moat and a new statement was issued. It gave an insight into the escalation of the hunt:

Monday, 5 July shootings – 07:30 update
Officers are continuing to search for Raoul Thomas Moat, 37, following three shootings in Gateshead and Newcastle.

Overnight police have been conducting additional patrols in specific areas across the force. Northumbria Police has called in mutual aid, requesting additional firearms trained officers from a number of other forces including Cleveland, Humberside, West Yorkshire, South Yorkshire and Cumbria in order to maximise the resources available.

The two people injured in the shootings Samantha Stobbart, 22, and PC David Rathband, 42, both remain in hospital. Both are described this morning as critical but stable.

Overnight a large scale operation has been launched involving a large number of officers including specialist search teams, armed response units, force helicopter and dog handlers who have been taking part in a co-ordinated response.

Officers have been contacting people Moat has been known to associate with, speaking to them to see if they can assist with the search. This is a methodical operation which has officers working to collate information from a wide range of sources.

This operation together with high profile patrols with officers fully briefed to locate Moat is ongoing. These efforts together with the large scale media response has played a major part in making the public aware of the police operation.

The search for Moat was already operating at a high level and after the shooting of PC Rathband, helicopters swept the city in the hope of finding a trace of the gunman and his vehicle.

At one stage, a report of a possible sighting came in of a man fitting Moat's description on the Ponteland Road in Newcastle, about a mile-and-a-half from Moat's house. The police helicopter was despatched and the man located; he was picked out by the searchlight and an armed team pounced, forcing him to the ground and pinning his arm behind his back whilst his identity was checked.

The man held face down on the pavement was a twenty-eight-year-old factory worker, who, after a night out with friends, was admittedly less than sober. He was relieved to hear one of the armed officers say: 'No, it's not him,' and was sent on his way, but this single incident was just one of several actions carried out throughout the early hours of the morning.

Temporary Chief Constable Sue Sim, said: 'All available officers, including a number from other forces, have been actively involved in the sustained search for Moat. This activity will continue as we are determined to find this man to draw an end to these violent events.

'We are still appealing for help from the public, if anyone knows where this man is we urgently need them to contact us straightaway. Friends who may think they are helping him are merely prolonging this situation which we need to safely resolve.

'Innocent people have been shot, one killed and two others seriously wounded and these events have shocked local people. Officers are working hard to track this man down and this work will continue until we are successful.'

Sim then stressed that although Moat was armed and at large, that the threat to the public was not thought at that stage to be significant. She said: 'Police do not believe him to be a general threat to the public at large, he has specific grievances against certain individuals and groups, however, the advice remains the same, if you see him do not approach him but call the police straightaway.'

To give an insight into the usual tasks of a press office, other releases at this time dealt with a request for witnesses to come forward if they had information about a fire at Newbiggin quarry and a report about the theft of a horse ornament in Morpeth. When an incident of the magnitude of the Moat shootings occurs, all personnel and resources are thrown into a wholly different gear. It is a rare event and almost impossible to plan for, but Newcastle was now the focus of UK-wide attention and requests were coming into the press office at an unprecedented volume.

Coordinating the search for Moat was a mammoth task and once the news filtered through that staff at Durham Prison had submitted a Security Information Report that included the concern that Moat might pose a threat to his ex-girlfriend, that undertaking became yet more complex. A press conference was convened at the force's headquarters in Ponteland and Temporary Chief Constable Sue Sim announced that the matter had been voluntarily referred to the IPCC. Ms Sim Said: 'Northumbria Police were not informed that Mr Moat intended to shoot or kill Samantha Stobbart. We were informed on Friday afternoon by Durham Prison that Mr Moat may intend to cause serious harm to his partner.

'We acknowledge that it is important that these matters are investigated thoroughly and I have voluntarily referred this aspect to the Independent Police Complaints Commission and we will, of course, fully cooperate with the Independent Police Complaints Commission.'

Pressure was building. Professor David Wilson, a former prison governor and now an academic at Birmingham City University, told the BBC: 'If there was intelligence which suggested that Moat was threatening his ex-partner and other members of the public, that matter should have been taken very seriously by Northumbria Police.'

In some ways, the voluntary referral to the IPCC by Northumbria had the effect of relieving some of that pressure and scrutiny on the force. As the matter was now under investigation, it was subject to the usual reporting restraints. Investigators from the IPCC were tasked with focusing on what information passed between prison staff, probation officers and police. It will be the IPCC that will rule on whether appropriate resources were allocated to handling the risk Moat posed, based on what people knew at the time.

The press had a field day highlighting the existence of the Security Information Report, suggesting that the police had been 'warned' about Moat. As pressure built to apprehend Moat, Sam's Stobbart's half-sister Kelly Stobbart said that 'nothing is going to stop Raoul'. She also described him as 'a man on a rampage' and there was little to dissuade anyone that she was wrong at that point. He was a gunman on the loose, prepared to kill and kill again.

It was a perilous operation for Northumbria police and coping with press attention and speculation was but one aspect of the complex enquiry. The decision was made to appeal to Moat once again. Through his use of letters and calls, it was clear that Moat had a strong desire to justify his actions and to be understood and so an attempt to communicate with him could be beneficial.

Sue Sim was to become a nationwide figure and, in contrast to her male colleagues, a good deal of attention would focus on her appearance. But it was Detective Chief Superintendent Neil Adamson who read out a direct appeal to Moat. It was the start of the force's attempted to create a dialogue and a rapport with the man who had seriously injured one officer and was intent on killing others.

Adamson said: 'Mr Moat, we are aware that you have a number of issues and grievances, some are very private, others relate to how you feel that you've been treated by us. We want to understand your position. And I want you to realise that you do have a future. We can only help you with this if you make contact with us directly.

'We've spoken to Sam and she has asked us to say the following to you. "Please give yourself up. If you still love me and our baby, you would not be doing this anymore." Sam also said: "When you came out of gaol, I told you that I was seeing a police officer. I said this because I was frightened. I have not been seeing a police officer."

'Mr Moat I know that you don't trust the police as you've told us that. So that you know that this message is genuinely from Sam she's told us about the Links of London chain bracelet that you bought her for Christmas. Please make contact with us.'

The signs that the police were taking advice from experts with a background in psychology are clear. By addressing the perpetrator as 'Mr Moat' and stressing the desire that they 'understand your position', Adamson was presenting the police in a respectful and even passive tone, something designed to appeal to Moat's sense of renewed self-importance since he'd acted out his threats.

The key information the police wanted to relay was that Chris Brown was not, nor ever had been, a police officer. The suggestion that Mr Brown was on the force had inadvertently inflamed Moat, and there was a very urgent need for the police to clarify that it had not been true. The aim was that Moat would then reassess the degree of his hatred for, and desire to, inflict further injury towards other officers. The message from Sam was cleverly crafted too, by focusing on love, their baby, and a gift that Moat had given Sam at Christmas. The hope was that Moat would snap out of what had been described by witnesses to the murder of Chris Brown as an almost hypnotic state of absence of animation or 'blankness'.

That is where talk of the 'future' became important. Once the reality of Moat's actions and likely endgame became apparent to an already unstable man, the result could be bloody. Either he'd simply kill himself, or, in a

Above: Officers search for Raoul Moat in the surrounding areas of Northumberland during the first week of July 2010.

Below: Police forensics at the scene of the first incident involving Moat in Birtley, Gateshead.

Above: The village of Rothbury in Northumberland was the scene of Moat's stand-off with police on 10th July 2010.

Below: Police search the ground following Moat's attack on PC David Rathband on 4th July 2010.

Police in Rothbury, Northumberland, during the search for Moat in July.

Above: Northumbria Police Temporary Chief Constable Sue Sim and Detective Chief Superintendent Neil Adamson speak to the media at Northumbria Police HQ.

Below: Police search the area in and around Rothbury, Northumberland.

Above: Officers outside a bakery during the search for Raoul Moat.

Below: Police surround Moat during the stand-off on the banks of River Coquet.

Above: A storm drain in Rothbury, alleged to have been used by Moat.

Below: The area beside the River Coquet where it is believed the stand-off with Moat took place.

Police forensics conduct investigations following Moat's death on 10th July 2010.

Above: Officers from the Northumberland Police Marine Unit search the river and bank side following Moat's death.

Below: Raoul Moat's brother, Angus, reads a statement to the press following his brother's funeral.

final blaze of retributive fury, do so and also take as many others with him as possible.

Again, it is worth remembering that Derrick Bird had ended his horrific spate of murders only four weeks earlier. The prospect that another armed 'madman' was on the loose in the county that bordered Cumbria was a terrifying prospect.

PC David Rathband was still in a critical condition but was said to be in remarkable spirits. There was a surge in public sympathy for the officer who, although out of immediate danger, had suffered horrifying injuries.

In the midst of the largest British manhunt in living memory, one that had already mobilised officers from across six forces and a number of armed response units, the death of Chris Brown was to a certain degree forgotten. Not by his many friends and his family: his mother and sister were devastated by the loss. Chris was only 29 years old, a much loved son, brother, and a father-of-two, and someone who had known Samantha for only a brief period of time.

Neither had he been forgotten by the police. Since the enquiry into how the murder of teenager Stephen Lawrence was handled, a number of recommendations had been made and adopted by the force. One focused on how police support families during sudden death investigations and it is now standard practice that Family Liaison Officers are appointed to help support victims' families and to improve the flow of information between them and the investigative team. The officers are a main point of contact as families struggle to come to terms with a very traumatic event. An event for the Brown family that was being exacerbated by the media frenzy over Moat.

The police had advised Chris's family not to talk to the press in case it further enraged Moat and the enormity of the task ahead was clear to all involved. Violent death leaves families with an almost overwhelming legacy of grief and despair. Moat could not be allowed to bring yet more horror into the lives of others.

Samantha Stobbart was now under police protection: there was no telling if Moat would make another attempt on her life. The police did not know where the killer was but they did not think that he'd left the North East. He was close.

That evening, the police released the images of PC Rathband's blood-covered face. They were truly shocking and the public was left in no doubt what Moat was capable of. The hope was that anyone with information about Moat's whereabouts would be prompted to speak out.

PC Rathband had agreed that the images should be released and Sue Sim spoke for all his colleagues when she paid tribute to his professionalism and his courage. She said: 'Despite being seriously injured David demonstrated extreme bravery by alerting his colleagues and even managed to give fellow officers vital information about the incident, which has proved invaluable during the course of this investigation.

'I have nothing but absolute admiration for David. He acted in the best traditions of the police service, showing outstanding bravery in what must have been a terrifying situation.

'True to form, despite his horrific injuries, David has made it clear he wants us to catch the person responsible for this horrendous attack. Our thoughts remain with him, his family and colleagues at this extremely difficult time.'

What was not revealed at the time was that Sue Sim made a personal promise to David Rathband that everything possible would be done to prevent Moat from killing anyone else. It was a bold thing to promise but was a mark of the Temporary Chief Constable's implacable determination to apprehend the man.

Rolling news brought a new level of pressure to bear on the operation and Sim had expressed her disquiet about the negative impact that press coverage had on a huge news story from the past. In May 2009, she spoke before the House of Commons' Home Affairs Select Committee in her capacity as the spokesperson on public order issues for the Association of Chief Police Officers. The committee had convened to examine the events of 1 April that year when demonstrators took to the City of London as part of the G20 protests.

Demonstrators clashed with police and later that day

Ian Tomlinson, a newspaper vendor making his way home, had died. A postmortem report stated that Mr Tomlinson had died as a result of a heart attack but once *The Guardian* newspaper obtained video footage showing a police officer striking Mr Tomlinson with a baton and shoving him to the ground shortly before he collapsed, there was a public outcry.

Sue Sim told the committee that she did not believe in 'trial by press' and that media coverage could give a biased view of events. Her remarks were measured although they were greeted as 'unsatisfactory' by one of the MPs present. That the relationship between the police and the press can be difficult is nothing new but it is arguable that rolling news has made the task of managing any high profile enquiry more difficult.

There are those within the police who feel that the press are overtly critical, to quote one police blogger, Inspector Leviathan, from the Police Oracle: 'Hardly a day goes by without picking up a newspaper, turning on the television or listening to the radio, that there isn't an article, sound-bite or news-feed criticising the police service.'

It isn't always a harmonious relationship of course because what the press wants to use and what the police would like to see reported aren't always synchronised. The press can exacerbate matters as pages are filled or hours of coverage put to bed, but, as this case would go to show, cooperation isn't out of the question.

The media were soon to find another story to file as a report came in later that evening that an armed man had entered a fish-and-chip shop in nearby Seaton Delaval and demanded cash from the till. It had happened at around 10.50pm that evening in the North East coastal village that lies about nine miles to the west of Newcastle. The gunman was described as six foot tall, white and aged about 35 with a 'muscular build' and 'short sandy-coloured hair'. No one was hurt, cash was handed over and the man left. The feeling was that it had to be Moat.

The decision was made to release details about the car that the police suspected Moat had access to. The statement read:

Police have released details of a car believed to be associated with Raoul Thomas Moat.

The car is a black Lexus described as having a full body kit and two regular alloy wheels and two "space saver" thin wheels. Car model number IS200 SE a saloon. It is very noisy and has damage under its bumper at the front near side.

Superintendent Dennis Shotton added: 'We have information that this car is connected to Moat, although it does not belong to him but to an associate. We are keen to trace it as it may help us to locate Moat.'

And the car would be the key. Unbeknownst to the

police and to Moat, a local retiree always had an eye for a Lexus as she quite admired its design. She wasn't used to seeing one with a full body kit perhaps, but she had noticed such a car when she was walking her dogs. Mrs Wilson had set off with her husband, their Labrador and their spaniel for an evening stroll when she noticed a black Lexus parked on the side of the road. As she passed, she noticed that it had a plastic cover on the driver's seat and saw that it was a V reg. Cars were often parked there, it was a popular spot, close to the river and near to where people liked to camp.

After all, it was the time of year when Rothbury became busier than ever, as holiday-makers made their way to the town.

CHAPTER TEN
2003

It is not always possible to know what changes in life will be of little consequence and which ones will shift familiar boundaries.

Take the Private Security Industry Act of 2001. It opens by stating: 'Be it enacted by the Queen's most Excellent Majesty, by and with the advice and consent of the Lords Spiritual and Temporal, and Commons, in this present Parliament assembled, and by the authority of the same, as follows: ...'

Reading the introductory paragraph of the Act gives some sense of how arcane law-making can appear to ordinary citizens, men like Raoul Moat and others who worked 'on the doors', many of whom would not have known that it was an act that was to radically change their livelihood.

The legislation meant that the private security industry would become regulated, although it would take another two years before the body responsible for that regulation – the Security Industry Authority (SIA) – was set up. Its aims were simple enough: the SIA would raise standards across the industry by way of a system of licensing. The hope was that the negative connotations surrounding the world of 'bouncers' would become a thing of the past and public confidence would be improved once 'door supervisors' were sufficiently trained.

The night-time club and pub economy was a growing sector, worth billions of pounds a year, but it relied on cities to create the right environment to encourage late night spending. In 2003, another sweeping change would be heralded with The Licensing Act, allowing bars to set their own hours and aimed at fostering a more 'Continental approach' to licensing on the High Street. It meant more people would be out at night and they would be drinking for longer, and that, in turn, brought a new set of problems for managing antisocial behaviour.

There were huge opportunities for private companies and the new chairman of the SIA, Molly Meacher, realised the value of increased cooperation with the police and said: 'The police service increasingly recognises that the industry is an indispensable partner in helping to tackle crime and antisocial behaviour.'

But she didn't pull her punches when she set out what the organisation had to achieve: she said that another significant objective was to drive out crime from the industry.

The SIA knew what it was up against and after a period of research, summarised the hill it had to climb. 'Its consultations suggest that private security is often regarded as a grudge purchase, a commodity defined by price not quality; with limited recognition of standards or accreditation and training seen as a cost rather than an investment.'

Its summary continued: 'There is a vicious circle of low profitability leading to low spending on staff training and low pay, leading to high staff turnover and high recruitment costs. There is also a criminal element working within the industry which affects public confidence and safety.'

From the rarefied English of 'Be it enacted by the Queen's most Excellent Majesty...' the SIA had got to grips with everything that was rotten about the private security industry and changes were inevitable. It would mean licensing approved contractors, training, monitoring of compliance and also criminal record checks. That is not to say that anyone with a criminal record would no longer be able to work as a door supervisor, but the criteria was much tougher. For example no one with a sentence for a serious offence would be considered for employment in the industry unless they were clean for at least five years. Public confidence had to come first.

Those providing new training-based accreditations, very often former police officers, were not surprised to find a degree of resistance from established door supervisors. But the industry was changing fast; regulation opened the business up to those who may not have considered it before – for instance women, and students looking for an income.

There were long-standing supervisors who believed that no one could teach them anything about 'working the doors'. Yet other factors emerged as to why some were reluctant to undergo training. To gain credits, there were written as well as practical assignments, and one trainer has spoken about the need to deal with the fact that some of the burly men taking the exam will be functionally illiterate. Needless to say, it was an aspect that had to be handled sensitively; sometimes it became necessary to allocate someone to such a literacy-challenged trainee, in order to transcribe their answers onto the exam paper.

There were many in the trade who came to see the value of training and saw that their position on the doors would be enhanced. Others viewed regulation as intrusive, and yet another area of life that was being monitored and tightened up with regulations.

The police welcomed the initiative and it is an unspoken truth that the relationship between door supervisors and the police is a symbiotic one – the benefits of sharing information can have mutual benefits. One insight is that if serious drugs come into a club and dealers take root, guns will follow. Door supervisors talk to the police, as they have to protect their club, otherwise they are not doing their job properly.

Off the record, police officers do not expect to know about every minor infringement, but they do expect a flow of information should it be necessary. This isn't about being an 'informer', or to give these people their current title of 'Covert Human Intelligence Sources' as they appear on the police payroll. This relationship is on a different footing and is one that works in bars and clubs in major cities, week in, week out.

Moat saw the changes coming in and he was becoming ambivalent about his life on the doors. It had provided most of his opportunities to meet women, which was a good thing, but he wasn't wedded to the role. There were plenty of other things he enjoyed, such as like buying cars, doing them up and selling them on. He'd see the cars he wanted advertised and would travel with a friend to pick them up. The Toyota MR2 was a car he particularly favoured – he could renovate this model relatively easily, and they had a good resale value.

Things between him and Marissa weren't great. The couple were living together in North Kenton with their two young girls but there were frequent arguments. Later that year Moat found himself featured in the press and even *The Times* picked his story up. He never expected that and he was less than happy about how he had become the focus of attention.

Raoul had been at the gym when he'd taken a call from a friend of his. He was on his way back to the house, unaware that his daughter Chantelle had accidentally fallen from her third floor bedroom window. He described the discovery of what had happened as the worst moment of his life. He said: 'I looked down and she was just lying there motionless. I felt sick and thought for sure she was dead. When I got there I was relieved to see her moving, she was even trying to get up, and I just rushed over to her.'

It was incredibly fortunate that Chantelle had survived but even more so once doctors realised that her injuries were merely superficial cuts and bruises. He went on to say: 'Chantelle is a very big girl and very strong for her age. She had managed to pull her bed under the window – it's not a very big bed and she somehow managed to drag it across the room. She is, as I said, very strong for her age – I'm a nightclub bouncer, so maybe she gets it from me.'

Maybe she did. Strength was still very much a virtue to Moat but the accident put an added strain onto his relationship with Marissa. By the following year, Moat's attentions had strayed elsewhere again and, by New Year's Eve, he thought that for once fate was finally going to work in his favour.

He'd met Samantha before, had chatted to her previously when she was on a night out and he'd been working at

Liquid, a bar and nightclub. There's no doubt that, to Moat, this was the most significant relationship of his life. But it also has to be acknowledged that at 16, Samantha was very young to be in a relationship, particularly one with a man who was fifteen years her senior. He may have been guilty of sensing in her an idealised form of womanhood, someone he could mould and control, but there is little doubt that, to him, his adoration was complete. He wrote:

> We'd known each other for a few years prior to this as she used to go to Newcastle drinking and talked to me while I worked on the door of Liquid Bar in the Bigg Market. We became quite close.
>
> Sam was like no other and filled huge gaps in my life, and changed my view on life.
>
> Always in my adult life I have felt alone, estranged from my entire family, and needing to belong somewhere but never did.
>
> I used to try and fill this gap with beautiful women, but all relationships failed, as it was never enough. No matter how good the looks and personality, I wanted more, but I didn't know what.
>
> All my life I wanted death, hence the reason I took risks, made the worst kind of enemies and behaved the way I did.
>
> But now I had different thoughts. I wanted my life with Sam.

Someone who understood me and helped me be who I wanted to be. She was beautiful, sexy and the best company ever. We waited about two months before sleeping together which made it so much more special.

Moat fell for Sam but he also fell for the idea of a redemptive love. The notion that love can heal all is a powerful one but it is also flawed. Relationships between adults is necessarily conditional; it is not the unconditional love that a parent can give a child.

If a relationship is to survive, love is underpinned by patience, mutual trust, a willingness to compromise and accepting and supporting a life partner's right to their own feelings, friends, activities and opinions. If conflict arises, as it is sure to, partners in a healthy relationship work towards a resolution that is fair to both. It isn't easy and the first flush of romance can carry a couple for only so long.

For those who grew up in an environment without stable and unconditional love, forming healthy attachments as an adult can be difficult. It is also common that they are formed with unrealistic expectations. Moat wanted Sam to be his princess, someone who saw him as the strong protector he always wanted to be, someone who would never let him down. Fear of abandonment and vulnerability can be overwhelming but at the outset of the relationship, love appeared to deliver Moat from such anxieties. He was besotted with Sam.

Samantha was just beginning to find her way in the adult world and had found herself her first job, as a hairdresser. She was impressed by Moat: here was a man willing to be a gentleman and to be utterly devoted to her. At first they were inseparable, spending every spare moment together, whether that meant joining Moat when he was repairing cars, or taking time off and travelling to Rothbury. He loved the village and spoke about his hope that they would one day live there.

Moat treated Sam 'like a princess', showering her with gifts as well as attention, although not everyone in her family was convinced that his obvious devotion was healthy. Sam's stepfather, Paul Stobbart, was concerned that, as a much older man, Moat should be dating someone nearer his own age. What's more, his insistence that Sam spend all her free time with him worried Paul too.

But for Sam, this was her first love and Moat could do no wrong. If this was the honeymoon period, it lasting long enough for Sam to convince her parents that she was ready to move into Moat's flat in Kenton after they had been together for only a few months. Her family worried if it was the right thing to do and their anxieties grew when Sam began to see less and less of her old circle of friends.

Moat was possessive. If other men approached Sam when she was out at the club it could enrage him. He liked Sam to wear figure-hugging clothes and was proud of her but worried constantly that she would be unfaithful. There was a suggestion that he even set up a honeytrap for Sam, using a friend to chat her up to see if she would respond to his advances. To his horror she did, and he ended up threatening not just Sam but warned the friend off too. At the back of Moat's mind was always the fear that she would leave him, but his possessive and aggressive attempts to control Sam would spell the undoing of their relationship.

They would argue. Sam would leave but then become filled with remorse; Moat would talk her round again. Sam's half-sister Kelly spoke of the pattern that their relationship fell into. She said: 'He'd come round and soft soap her and she'd disappear off and then we'd not hear from her for days because we knew she'd gone back to him and she knew we'd tell her she was a fool for doing it.'

People wondered if the steroids or other illegal drugs he sometimes used were unbalancing him. He certainly seemed unstable at times and yet friends and neighbours also talk of how friendly and likeable Moat could be. All agree, however, that they would not wish to cross him. But to Moat, Sam was 'the one' and he was sure that whatever their ups and downs, they were meant to be together forever.

CHAPTER ELEVEN

ESCAPE
TUESDAY 6 JULY

*The public need not fear me but the police should
as I won't stop till I'm dead.*
– from Raoul Moat's letters

Something had broken. Newsrooms checking the overnight updates from the police saw the sharp change of gear.

The task of managing an enquiry on such a scale is difficult and highly complex. On average, there were three hundred and fifty calls coming in to the police for each day that Raoul Moat was on the run. Some of them were suspected sightings and others offered possible 'intelligence' about his movements. A proportion of the callers were simply mistaken about what they saw but each call had to be followed up and the man-hours such work demands can surprise outsiders.

Taking statements is a laborious process and information has to be logged, updated and prioritised, depending on the direction of what was described even by modern policing as a 'fast moving and complex operation'.

In an ordinary murder enquiry, as well as taking statements from witnesses, a system of TIEs is used; in essence, this means that each person of interest has to be traced, interviewed and eliminated as a suspect. Information is cross-referenced against verifiable facts. At this stage, Moat was still wanted for questioning over the shootings in Birtley and the attack on PC Rathband but by now, this enquiry had far exceeded the boundaries of an ordinary murder investigation. It was a full-scale and multi-agency operation of unprecedented scale for Northumbria.

On the 'overnight' of 5 July, the press release demonstrated the art of revealing very little about a very tough operation. It read:

Dated: 05 Jul 2010
Following the shootings on Tyneside this weekend, police are continuing to search for Raoul Thomas Moat, 37.

Overnight police have been conducting additional patrols in specific areas across the force and carrying out intelligence led operations. Northumbria Police

has called in mutual aid, requesting additional
firearms trained officers from a number of
other forces.

There is no change to the condition of the two
people injured in the shootings, Samantha Stobbart,
22, and PC David Rathband, 42, both remain
in hospital.

Enquiries are ongoing and police continue to carry
out high profile patrols.

The statement was brief because the only thing that could be said was that all that should be done was being done. But a call from a couple in Rothbury changed everything. It was early but Mrs Wilson was watching breakfast news updates and noticed the details of the missing black Lexus on news reports about Moat. She picked up the phone and called the police, reasoning that the car may still be where it was parked when she'd seen it, and might be of interest.

The press conference scheduled for that morning was put back until 11.30am, but minutes before, the story broke.

A police statement read as follows:

Urgent advice for people in Rothbury area
Dated: 06 Jul 2010
This is an update on ongoing operational activity
taking place in the Rothbury area in connection with
the search for Raoul Thomas Moat.

As a precautionary measure we are closing down a geographic area near Rothbury. This is a two mile radial exclusion zone on the ground. In addition there is a five mile, 5,000 feet air exclusion zone.

Numerous resources are being deployed to the area to reassure the public and to carry out an effective search.

The public may experience some disruption and we are seeking their patience and co-operation.

Members of the public in this area are advised to remain indoors and await further instructions. Anyone considering visiting Rothbury is also advised not to travel at this stage.

People will see armed officers on the streets. This is a precautionary measure to protect and reassure them.

The air exclusion zone was designed to keep press helicopters out of the area and so it was clear that the village would be the focus for that day at least. Press teams scrambled into action – the police would have to contend with their arrival come what may. The 2-mile zone could also have been implemented as a result of Moat's use of one of his mobile phones. Mobile telephone service providers can locate the nearest telephone mast to the phone within two kilometres or so, if it has been switched on.

Just over ninety minutes earlier, what Detective Chief Superintendent Adamson described as 'one of a continuing number of firearms operations' had resulted in the police taking possession of the Lexus they had been looking for. It was unoccupied but the discovery was a breakthrough.

Moat, however, was still nowhere to be found. Adamson renewed his appeal for him to come forward, saying: 'Mr Moat, I have a further message for you. I have made a number of requests to you, to contact police and hand yourself in. That opportunity still exists.

'Please remember what I've said to you before. Don't leave your children with distressing memories of their father. You still have a future. Give yourself up now.'

He also remarked that he was 'confident that we are closing the net on Moat'. There was no 'Mr Moat' in this part of the statement and it was clear that this was a push and pull approach. Moat no longer had the upper hand. Police wanted him to read between the lines and know that, as he was Britain's most wanted man, time was running out.

What Detective Chief Superintendent Adamson also revealed that morning was how the media had been recruited in the first of two media blackouts. To add to the complications in an already difficult enquiry, he made public that his team had also been dealing with a 'complex, fast-moving and challenging hostage situation'. In his letter, Moat had suggested that he may have hostages with him. Adamson added that his team dealt with that development 'in accordance with national guidelines in relation to kidnap'.

The police have developed a range of procedural guidelines over the last twenty years and some of these pertain to kidnapping and extortion.

Little more can be said at this stage as the investigation into what did or didn't happen is still ongoing. But the situation does provide an insight into another difficult strand of the operation. It also shows that the media do work with the police if advised that any reporting could jeopardise a situation where there is a 'risk to life'. Adamson thanked the media publicly and, unbeknownst to those gathered at the briefing, it would not be the only time the press would have to agree to a voluntary blackout in the days ahead.

The enquiry was moving at an extraordinary rate. One further revelation came at the same briefing when Adamson stated that 'there is no reason at this stage' to link the fish-and-chip shop robbery at Seaton Delaval to Moat. Technically, it was possible that the car that Mrs Wilson saw parked at Rothbury at 9pm could have been driven to the coastal village – it is a distance of less that thirty miles but takes almost an hour due to the nature of the roads, and the robbery did not take place until 10.50pm. But if the robbery was unconnected to Moat, perhaps he arrived in Rothbury and, more importantly, maybe he was still there.

In the town of Rothbury, the contrast between local residents out picking up bread and milk and walking their dogs in the sunshine, and the sound of police helicopters plus the abrupt arrival of numbers of police vehicles on the streets became acute. A police Landrover drove through the High Street with a megaphone announcing that 'The police are here to protect you.' The difficulties in managing an operation in a residential area are obvious: the police have the almost impossible task of providing protection for the public without inducing a state of panic.

The public were advised to stay off the streets and most complied. The local butcher expressed the concerns of most residents when he told a reporter: 'It's a small rural town, it's not a thing we are used to. We've just seen this tragedy unfold in Cumbria and you think that could never happen here.' Derrick Bird had driven around the countryside of neighbouring Cumbria for three-and-a-half hours shooting people he selected at random before turning the gun on himself. The potential risk to those anywhere near Moat was obvious should his thoughts turn from targeting the police to turning his fire against members of the public. His letters stated that the public need not fear him but, as the net closed, who knew what he was capable of if he was sufficiently agitated?

Trying to create a picture of the type of man the police were dealing with was another part of the puzzle. When police are attempting to apprehend a killer, psychologists do draw up profiles for enquiry teams, but senior investigating officers use them only to give them a possible insight – there is nothing hard and fast that can be relied on except verifiable facts.

The profile that was drawn up for Adamson's team to a certain extent told the police what they already knew. It said: 'There is evidence to support the following antisocial personality traits – irritability and aggressiveness. He has demonstrated a long-standing belief that the police, with the assistance of other agencies, have persecuted and harassed him.'

But the key insight was this: 'He does demonstrate rigid and inflexible thinking with a failure to consider all potential solutions to the problem he faces.' That lay at the heart of Moat's brittle and tortured thinking. He could not see a way out, his fear and fury had overwhelmed him and he had abandoned any hope he'd nurtured of becoming the man and the father he wanted to be.

Part of the search now focused on the area around where the Lexus had been found, to the east of the village. There was woodland close by and although no camping was allowed there, locals knew that it was sometimes used by tent-dwellers illegally. Staff working out of the industrial estate could see armed police enter the wood and they were advised to lock the doors to their buildings. For those working there who were also parents, concern then turned to the local schools. So many people were calling that the phone lines were continually engaged. The school day would not finish for another three hours, but the prospect that Moat could target the three local schools left parents in a quandary as to what to do.

Armed police began to search a disused farmhouse as a helicopter hovered overhead. Seeing armed officers and marksmen with police dogs and body armour is still a rarity on the streets outside major cities, and suddenly this kind of personnel seemed to be in the town in unprecedented numbers.

In fact, the workload of armed response officers has increased dramatically over the last 10 years, particularly in major cities, and their role has been finessed. Officers in Armed Response Vehicles are trained to respond quickly to events as they unfold and typically they are crewed by three officers, each with a specific function. The driver's task is to get the crew to the scene in the fastest, safest way possible; the 'operator' is responsible for the in-car communications and trying to glean as much information as possible before they arrive at the scene; and the 'observer' travels in the rear of the vehicle and provides the driver with suitable route updates.

Once they arrive at the scene, the officers make an immediate assessment. If an 'armed containment' is required to isolate an armed suspect, two of the crew will deploy, leaving one to control the incident and call for further armed support. In Moat's case, searches were carried out with enough officers to operate a 'containment' but he had yet to be traced.

Officers were armed with Glock 17 self-loading pistols and others also had Heckler and Koch MP5 carbines. Supervising officers from the firearms department take charge of the armed officers and they carry additional equipment, such as items needed to gain a forced entry to premises. Specialist Firearms Officers (SFOs) were also on hand to provide 'an enhanced firearms capability'. These officers undergo advanced firearms training, including how to run pre-planned operations and instructions for managing a hostage-rescue capability.

Despite the sudden and intense activity in the town, police were also carrying out operations in and around Newcastle too. A house in Wrekenton, in Gateshead, was raided; it was thought to belong to a friend of Moat's.

Rumours were circulating at an even faster pace. Moat was armed with at least two guns and was well stocked with ammunition. It was the kind of story that can fuel hysteria and police were dealing with yet another swell in phone calls from the public. A report of a man 'jumping off a hay bale' near the school in Rothbury was typical, at once demanding a response, since the jumper could be Moat, while on the other hand, might be soaking up resources when they might be needed elsewhere if it turned out to be a false alarm.

As a precautionary measure, the school was instructed not to send children home until the area was secured. In the mind of every parent was the horror of the Dunblane shootings, the possibility that a malcontent with a desire to inflict pain was once again armed and in a rural village. The school was placed under police protection and, inside the building, curtains and blinds were drawn and teachers did their best to calm the children. The two other schools in Rothbury also received police protection.

The question of resources was even raised in the House of Commons and the Home Secretary, Theresa May, said: 'I have spoken to Acting Chief Constable Sue Sim and Home Office officials will remain in regular contact with the force.

Northumbria Police are being supported by other forces and I am confident everything possible is being done to catch the suspect. We are available to discuss any additional support and assistance Northumbria Police may need.'

Whilst that statement may sound reassuring it is also an indication of the squeeze senior officers must feel once a local incident becomes a national and even a global story. The pressure to catch Moat, who could be hiding anywhere in a region as large as a national park, grew by the hour and the policing bill would stretch into the millions.

One of Moat's ex-girlfriends gave an interview to the press saying that she'd often been camping with him in and around Rothbury when they were in their early twenties, and she said that not only did Moat know the area 'like the back of his hand' but that the numerous nooks and crannies meant that he could hide out for days. As she spoke, more armed searches were underway in disused buildings and the old railway that used to serve the town. Tensions were running high and it was not until 5pm that the police felt confident enough to allow children to leave the school.

Another press conference was scheduled for early evening and those used to driving in to Rothbury after a day working in the city found that they could not enter the town but instead were directed to a school in nearby Longhorsley that would have to serve as a temporary place of shelter.

It wasn't Sue Sim or Neil Adamson, the two faces most closely connected to the operation, that led that evening's press briefing but Chief Superintendent Mark Dennett, area commander for Northumberland. He said to those gathered: 'Members of the public are advised to remain indoors and await further instructions. Also anyone visiting Rothbury is advised not to travel at this stage.

'Raoul Thomas Moat is still potentially at large and we are undertaking a search in what is a significant and challenging geographic area and it may take several hours. There are armed officers on the streets of Rothbury and we understand this may concern people but this is a precautionary measure to protect and reassure them.'

The streets of the town were empty, and whether its residents were reassured or not was hard to know. A family that had been out all day called the police as they feared that an intruder had broken in. The mother who had returned with her two young children noticed straightaway that food had been taken. As a precaution, she called the police and took her children out of the house. As she was leaving, she thought she heard a noise coming from a closed bedroom door.

An armed response unit was sent in but no one was found. The mother was too worried to sleep there that night and stayed with friends. However, the house was not watched over, and later someone broke into it again. Someone had even slept in the spare bed.

The highly visible police presence was designed to reassure the community as well as play a part in the search for Moat. But no one now was sure that Moat would be caught that night. With remote farm outbuildings and the woods to hide in, the men hunting him were not sure either.

CHAPTER TWELVE
2005

It might not have been a vintage year for the programme but the sixth series of *Big Brother* did at least boast a winner from the North East. Anthony Hutton from Consett in County Durham, a 1970s dancer, told the show's presenter Davina McCall: 'I haven't got the vocabulary to describe how I feel but I feel absolutely mint.'

Almost seven million people watched the final, more than the number of people who had tuned in to see the Live 8 concerts a month earlier on BBC One. Over a million pounds changed hands as bets were placed before the final and it was Hutton who walked away with £50,000. A dancer, Hutton went on to star in Christmas

Panto in Darlington and released a keep fit DVD called *Anthony's 70's Disco Workout* and Council leader, Alex Watson said: 'Anthony has certainly put Consett on the map.'

Since the programme first aired in 2000, *Big Brother* had become a huge hit, sometimes attracting almost half the available TV audience, and it was proving particularly popular with the demographic that was increasingly hard to attract – young men and women. Advertisers loved it because the under-30s relished the programme, even if the reason why it was a hit wasn't always clear. What had started as a fairly sober 'social experiment' became an entertainment phenomenon showing 'ordinary' people chosen, it seemed, for displaying ever more eccentric behaviour. Despite column inches condemning the programme, its appeal was clear. One online fan summed it up: 'Because every person can show his talents and get easy fame.'

Easy fame was the promise not just of *Big Brother* but other reality shows such as *Pop Idol* and *X Factor*. However as 'talent' shows contestants were expected to have some skills – even though it was those with least talent that often provided the greatest entertainment. It was *Big Brother* that fostered the greatest novel idea, that being 'ordinary' was a gift in itself, as the meteoric rise of the show's 2003 contestant, Jade Goody, had shown.

From being pilloried by the press, and voted 'fourth

worst Briton' in a Channel 4 poll, Jade went on to publish an autobiography, create a best-selling perfume, make over £2m and by 2007 was ranked twenty-fifth in a poll of the most influential people in the world by *Heat* magazine. Such transformations were possible, and it seemed that an audience would cheer on those exposed in the media who were willing to unashamedly share their life story.

Raoul Moat gave little thought to Anthony Hutton that year however, as he had more to worry about. He had been stopped by the police as he drove a Mitsubishi Colt through Newcastle, although the vehicle wasn't his. Officers searched the car and discovered a cobra-headed Samurai sword in the boot and a twin-bladed knuckleduster hidden beneath the dashboard.

Moat admitted that the sword belonged to him but denied knowing anything about the knuckleduster. When the case came to court, the accused said that the sword was in the car as he was on his way to try and sell the weapon, deciding to get rid of it because his daughter didn't like the snake detailing on it. He said: 'She does not like snakes, so I wanted to get rid of it.'

The daughter he was referring to was one from his previous relationship with Marissa. The couple were not on good terms but Moat still maintained contact with his girls. One friend spoke of Moat's devotion to them saying that he 'lived for his children'. The same man spoke of Raoul's faults but saw the best in him, talking of the good times that they enjoyed, working together and 'getting wrecked off our nuts'. The pictures that would later appear to show Moat in a woman's dress was one result of such a night out. Raoul's friend explained that they had all messed around, attempting to make each other laugh by performing increasingly daft antics. The Raoul Moat that would come to dominate the headlines was not a man he recognised.

How the two men met however, is telling. The man, let's call him John, and his girlfriend were kept awake over many nights by a neighbour playing loud music. Eventually, John lost his patience and told the nuisance neighbour that if it wasn't turned down, he'd rip the sound system from the wall. It was turned down, for thirty minutes. Hearing it at full volume again, John entered the flat, only to find that his neighbour had clearly called for back-up in the form of two very large men, one of whom was Moat. John had made the threat to pull the player from the wall and knew that he couldn't back down. There was 'an altercation' but John had made his point. He could not be seen to capitulate.

Some time later, after moving, John found that he and Moat were neighbours and, through a mutual acquaintance, they met and it was a start of their friendship. He knew about the arrest over the sword but also spoke of Moat's deteriorating relationships with the authorities.

It was said that after Chantelle fell out of the window, he had threatened council workers who fitted window locks to his property, a claim Moat denied. He went on record saying: 'In my line of work you lose your job if you're abusive or lash out, so you learn how to control your temper.'

The police were another matter. John believes that Moat was subject to unfair attention, claiming that he knew of a number of occasions when his friend was pulled over by police and also that when his own car was parked on the street without a valid tax disc, he wasn't ticketed, whereas Moat's vehicles were.

The impression may well have been a false one but it was enough for Moat to vocalise his irritation with authority. He felt he was being singled out and by the time he moved with Sam to a new area, he wanted to ensure that he would not be misrepresented again. He would install CCTV cameras and begin to tape conversations. That way, he'd have proof of exactly what was going on.

It was another attempt to gain control over a life he sometimes felt was slipping through his hands. It was hard enough to keep his head above water and keep his relationship with Sam on track but then Sam had news that he was sure would mean a fresh start. She was pregnant. He was thrilled to learn that he'd be a father again and this time, he was adamant that everything would change. He would change, life would change. It would all be good.

He wanted to find a new home for them but another thought had taken hold too. He wanted his other daughters to live under his roof, not Marissa's. It would mean a bitter custody dispute but he was willing to fight for control over his girls.

Marissa has since spoken of the months that led up to the decision as to where the girls should live and has said that Raoul would stop at nothing to get his way. She said: 'I have been accused of dealing drugs, keeping guns and neglecting my children, but it was all lies. Raoul painted the worst possible picture of me and people believed that I was a terrible mother.' Marissa sensed that the tide was turning against her and felt that Moat was determined to destroy her. She claimed that the police arrived at her home searching for drugs and firearms after an anonymous caller suggested that she had these items hidden at her property. Even the RSPCA were called after a tip-off that she might be mistreating her dog.

At the heart of the conflict Marissa believed that Moat was behaving as he was in a desire to make her life a misery. She claims that even after they had separated, he made threats against her life, should she start dating anyone else.

Moat knew what a childhood could be like growing up without a father and he was adamant that he would remain a central figure in his children's lives. He also knew how fragile relationships could be, as he had not been in touch with his brother or mother for some time. He had drifted away from them and did not know when he'd have cause to speak to them again. Well aware of other people's circumstances however, Moat knew that his situation was not that uncommon.

A lot of those he came across grew up without a parent, or had children that they didn't see because of conflict with an ex, or by simply because they lost touch. It was common for relationships to break down, he realised, it was just the way it was and there was no point in complaining. Moat reasoned that he would just have to get to grips with it all. In his mind it was simple. His children would all live with him and he and Sam would complete the family he had always wanted.

CHAPTER THIRTEEN

CLOSING THE NET
WEDNESDAY 7 JULY

Raoul, son, please this has to stop, we don't want anyone else hurt, nee more son.
– from an appeal made by Paul Stobbart

The rain that had fallen heavily in the night had hampered efforts to search for Moat during the hours of darkness, and for those tracking him, the prevailing reasoning would have been that any discomfort they encountered from the elements would be mirrored, or even magnified, for Moat.

Adrenalin can take you only so far – hunger and exhaustion wear away even those trained and hardened to perform covert operations in the wilderness. Someone who knew Moat well spoke of how he'd normally eat five substantial meals a day, far more food than he'd be able to find scavenging or carrying about with him. For the police, this was also a waiting game.

Moat would have to surface soon; he could not remain immobile or unsupported indefinitely. And the pursuers had another breakthrough – they found a tent that Moat had been using. It was discovered after a local family reported seeing smoke rising from what was probably a camp fire, near a farm on the outskirts of Rothbury. Inside was an eight page letter addressed to Samantha.

Letters were obviously important to Moat and mimicking this trait of his, the police put together a missive of their own that was distributed to the hunted man's friends and associates, in case one of them received a visit from Moat, as Andy McAllister had. Written on Northumbria police headed notepaper it stated: 'Raoul. Early on Sunday morning you contacted us on two occasions by dialling 999 and told us about what you had done and why you did these things.

'You told us how angry you were and you also told us that you were sorry that Sam had been so seriously hurt. We understand how personal and important these things are to you.

'We want you to contact us again as soon as you are able so we can discuss these things with you and provide you with a full update on how Sam is.'

It was aimed to appeal to Moat's desperation to discover

more about Sam's condition and it was a sign that police were now being proactive in reaching out to Moat in new ways. Overall, there was the gathering sense that the police were beginning to get on top of the search for the fugitive. Restrictions on the village of Rothbury were relaxed from the high state of readiness seen the day before. Parents were advised that children could be safely walked to the schools, which were open. The roads were open too, even though vehicles were being checked as they came in and out of the village.

The police released a statement conveying the hope that residents were confident in the way the operation was being conducted and assuring them that every effort was being made to minimise its impact on their lives. It read:

Northumbria Police is continuing to search for Raoul Thomas Moat, and this systematic operation is ongoing during the hours of darkness.

Temporary/Deputy Chief Constable Jim Campbell said: 'We are committed to doing all we can to find this man which means the intensive and systematic searches are continuing throughout the night. Armed officers remain in the town and will work on.

'We want to reassure residents in the Rothbury area that despite this activity it is still very much 'business as usual' for local residents. Schools in

Rothbury will be fully open on Wednesday and police resources will be in place to reassure parents that they can safely take their children to and from school. Local residents are being encouraged to go about their normal business.

'The stringent two mile exclusion zone has now been down graded. This means that while police officers will still be patrolling the area, residents and visitors, and their vehicles, may be checked by officers coming into the town and also when they leave.

'We will continue to keep a large and highly visible police presence in the town of Rothbury for as long as necessary while the search continues.

'We do need help from the public to be vigilant and to report any suspicious incidents to us immediately. Then we can respond and take any necessary action.

'We recognise that this large scale police presence has interrupted normal life for many people and we want to reassure residents that we are doing all we can to bring this investigation to a conclusion.'

Although there was a measured and calm tone used in the release, in reality the search had intensified. A Metropolitan Police spokesperson said: 'We are sending a specialist firearms officer team, which includes some rifle officers. We are also sending some eight armed response vehicles, which carry three officers in each. They are equipped with regular MP5 weapons.'

A request for assistance had also gone to the Police Service of Northern Ireland and they confirmed that twenty armoured cars would be driven to Northumbria for officers to use. At first this conjured up alarming images of armoured vehicles patrolling the streets, but in reality the cars were in fact Mitsubishi Shoguns: 4x4s that appear 'normal' but are fitted with added protection to help make them bulletproof.

When it came to monitoring the roads, in many respects the task at Rothbury was fairly straightforward. The likely route that Moat would have travelled from Newcastle would have taken him along the A1 and towards one of the three B roads that meet at the village. At one point on the journey there, Moat would have passed a sign that reads: 'Police. Unmarked Cars Operating' and his reaction can only be guessed at.

He must have known that his options were running out. In shooting a policeman, he had crossed a line and joined that grizzly list of men who will always be tirelessly pursued by the law.

In 1966 career-criminal Harry Roberts shot and killed three police officers who'd stopped him in his car. He panicked because there were guns in his vehicle that had been used in a previous armed robbery. Roberts went on the run and made his way to Epping Forest, and, echoing the reasons why Moat fled to the countryside, chose the place because he knew the area well from spells spent there in childhood.

Roberts evaded capture for 96 days and although he was camping out and sleeping rough, he also used to nip into a café to eat — not in itself remarkable until it was realised that the eatery was adjacent to a police station. After capture he was tried and imprisoned and then he became an antihero to some, with his name being chanted on football terraces. He is now one of Britain's longest serving prisoners.

Yet perhaps it was a more recent manhunt that had the greatest parallels with the puruit of Moat. In the summer of 1982, Barry Prudom went on the run after shooting a police officer. The manhunt was huge, involving over a thousand officers from 12 forces. Some who took part in the search for Prudom have since talked of the eerie tension that built as they fanned through the forest at night, knowing that the killer could have been watching them.

After 12 days on the run the fugitive walked into the Yorkshire town of Old Malton and killed another officer on patrol. He had already shot another man dead, injured his wife, and later would take an elderly father and son hostage. The old man had the presence of mind to strike up a rapport with Prudom, who eventually left them unharmed, even addressing the old man several times as 'Dad'.

A police cordon was thrown around Malton but Prudom escaped. Like Moat, Prudom was also a man who loved the outdoors, but this would prove his undoing. He'd taken an outdoor survival course with Eddie McGee, a survival expert who'd served with the Parachute Regiment and the SAS. McGee had two sons serving as police officers in Yorkshire and he agreed to help track his former student. On day 17, Prudom was eventually cornered and he turned the gun on himself. But on hearing the shot, police marksmen fired at their quarry. At the inquest, the jury reached a verdict of suicide.

After this man's death, facts emerged about his earlier life. He had never known his father although later his mother married and he had a stepfather from whom he took his surname. He did marry but his wife later walked out on him because he was violent and possessive. Prudom became the subject of a record by the controversial band Combat 84. The band's lead singer, Chris Henderson, wrote about the killer's exploits as a football hooligan, one of the notorious Chelsea Headhunters, and he included lyrics that arguably identified yet another antihero.

How Moat was viewed by the wider public was a factor relevant to the operation. This went beyond how any personal loyalties may have had a part to play in his evasion. There were those who knew Moat who urged him to give himself up, and one powerful appeal came from Sam's father, Paul Stobbart. He said: 'Raoul son, please, this has to stop. It's gone on far too long. What sort of memories are these that the kids will have of their father.

'If they ask me in the future, the bairns, I will tell them, exactly what's happened,' he continued. 'I won't lie to them, you know that. I don't want to have to tell them what might upset them, about you, or what ever has gone on. Howay son, give it up.'

Paul Stobbart was only five years older than Moat but in many ways he did represent a far more mature figure than that of Moat. He looked older, was not as concerned with his appearance, and had been a solid fixture in Sam's life for many years. He was a man of principle too, and a decade earlier he had led a convoy of fellow truck drivers from Birtley as part of the fuel tax protests. He'd been a protester at the Stanlow refinery blockade in Cheshire too and when the time came to take the convoy to London, he took his wife Lesley and daughter Samantha with him.

He told a reporter at the time about why he'd put a caravan in the back of his seven-ton lorry. He said: 'I usually have it in the field with the horses, like. It's got a shower, a toilet and a gas fire, its like a home from home. When you've got a wife and bairn you've got to get a wash, like.' The needs of his family always came first.

Paul Stobbart knew that there were times in life when you had to take a stand but Moat's actions were beyond him. He cared deeply about his family and was worried about the impact of Moat's violence on his youngest grandchild, Chanel. What kind of legacy had Moat created?

At the press conference that morning, the police were about to announce a £10,000 reward for information that led to Moat's detention. Detective Chief Superintendent Adamson would also reveal that the fugitive's tent had been found and stressed once again that Moat was mistaken in his belief that Chris Brown was a police officer.

Adamson also revealed that their enquiry into the robbery at the fish-and-chip shop at Seaton Delaval had now led them to believe that Moat was responsible. It was yet another twist in the saga but Adamson said that he sensed that Moat was still in Rothbury.

As Adamson wrapped up the briefing, Prime Minister David Cameron was making his comments about the operation in the House of Commons. He said: 'I know the House and the whole country will be wishing the police well in their search for this individual so that we can put a stop to the horrendous spree that is taking place.'

The story was by now not only dominating the local and national press coverage but was featuring online, specifically on Twitter. Trendsmap produces 'real-time' mapping of trends from traffic on Twitter across the world; they reported that across the North East, the words 'Raoul' and 'Moat' dominated. A local reporter in her twenties admitted that, for the first time, her friends took an interest in a story that she was covering. Moat was breaking though into that difficult-to-pin-down demographic, the twentysomethings. To some, he was an ordinary man caught in the glare of media attention, just like a *Big Brother* contestant. Only this was life and death.

There was more intriguing footage to come as the police were filmed marching a handcuffed man around several locations; his face was covered but he was wearing body armour. This guy was said to be an 'associate' of Moat's, helping police to search certain locations. One psychologist has spoken about this very visible 'parading' of a friend as having possibly been contrived, an attempt to allow Moat to hand himself in with honour in order to protect this person, as well as certain of his other friends who may have been caught up in the hunt. If it was the case that Moat was meant to see the images and consider handing himself in, it didn't work. However, it did provide the media with yet more powerful images to broadcast and print.

Moat was big news and the press had increased newspaper sales to prove it. Keeping the story fed with live updates was almost as big an operation as anything the police had mounted. The brutal truth is that, in part, Moat's escape was seen as fascinating to follow. The hunt was a form of news-as-entertainment. It was a trend that began when American actor O J Simpson set off on his white Ford Bronco across Orange County in 1994, providing news crews with over an hour of live footage of the chase and netted the TV station very high ratings.

Even across the space of just over an hour, the pursuit was long enough for spectators to come out onto the highway and watch, and some even had time to make banners cheering Simpson on. Some even described it as having the feeling of being a small-part actor in a film. The murders of Nicole Brown Simpson and Ronald Goldman four days earlier, and the reason why Simpson was supposed to hand himself in to the Los Angeles Police Department that day seemed to have been forgotten.

In a time of spectacle and excitement, painful human tragedies can be overlooked. It took Paul Stobbart to again remind everyone about some of what was at stake. He pleaded with Moat once more. He said, repeating some of his earlier sentiments: 'You know, Raoul, the children are number one, nothing will happen to them. I will make sure of that. What sort of legacy is this for your daughter?'

'You know I won't lie if she asks about her dad,' he went on, 'how good a dad you have been and how bad it has turned out. I want no one else hurt, this has gone too far. I am a family man and my heart is in bits. Please hand yourself in.'

CHAPTER FOURTEEN
2007
THURSDAY 1 JULY

'I wish everyone, friend or foe, well, and that is that. The end.' As last words go, they were perhaps not the most eloquent but they were enough to earn Tony Blair a standing ovation in the House of Commons; it was his final appearance at Prime Minister's Questions and he was handing over the reins to Gordon Brown after ten years in power.

There was a collegiate air of bantering and goodwill and he read out the details of his newly arrived P45 to gales of laughter: 'Details of employee leaving work. Surname: Blair; first name: T. It said actually: Mr, Mrs, Miss or other. This form is important to you, take good care of it, P45.'

Mr Blair, of course, would not have to worry too greatly

about his future prospects. In fact, he would go on to earn many millions in his role as a consultant and speech maker over the coming year: £2.5m from JP Morgan Chase alone. And of course he could rely on the £84,000 of taxpayers' money to run his private office plus his annual pension of £63,468.

The distance between the lives of those working in Westminster and the constituents they were elected to represent could sometimes appear as an un-bridgeable gulf. Take one of the houses Mr Blair bought as he planned for his retirement from politics: the house on Connaught Square in London, purchased for £3.65 million in 2004. This home contrasts sharply with the house he and his wife owned in his North East constituency of Sedgefield, an impressive four-bedroom detached house valued at £300,000. Yet as average house prices in the town stand at less than £95,000, even in Sedgefield the Blairs enjoyed a standard of living that was unattainable to most.

Of course, the counterpoint to that is to recognise that the Blairs achieved a great deal of their wealth through hard work and their careers in law, before Tony entered politics. Cherie has written about her 'ordinary' background growing up in Liverpool, yet in truth Mrs Blair was born in 1954, and hers was a generation that saw a great deal of upward mobility due to the opportunities that came to those who excelled at school and gained a place at a university in the 1970s.

Since then social mobility has ground to a halt. The hope that children from poorer backgrounds would grow to earn more than their parents has not materialised. In fact, in 2005, the Sutton Trust produced research that revealed a significant decline in upward mobility between those born in 1958 and those born in 1970. In essence, a child's life chances mirror those of its parents. In fact, the UK, alongside the United States, came bottom of the league of 11 developed countries that determined a child's chances of climbing the social or income ladder.

Two years later the Sutton Trust produced a follow-up report that showed that this lack of social mobility is now affecting generations not just born from the 1970s, but even those now born after the millennium. That covers both the generation that Moat was born to as well as that of his children.

Yet it was the Labour party under Blair's leadership that vowed to bridge the social divide. In 1999 he told the Labour Conference: 'If we are in politics for one thing, it is to make sure that all children are given the best chance in life.' Social inequality had grown in the 1980s and, for New Labour, the hope was that if access to higher education was radically expanded, more children from poorer backgrounds would be able to improve their life chances.

However, despite the expansion, by the late 1990s there had only been a three per cent increase in poorer children graduating from university, whilst their wealthier contemporaries took up 26 per cent of the available places. Furthermore, when it comes to taking up positions in professions at the higher end of the social scale, it would take the Milburn Report to expose how entrenched the elite and the privileged still are in the UK today.

Forty-five per cent of top civil servants, 50 per cent of doctors, 32 per cent of members of parliament, 53 per cent of top journalists, 70 per cent of finance directors and 75 per cent of judges come from the seven per cent of the population who went to private schools.

When the laissez-faire approach to economics took hold 30 years ago – allowing industry to be free of state intervention – it seemed that it had a direct consequence on the life chances of those at the lower end of the social ladder and in regions that were formerly reliant on the industrial and manufacturing base, as the North East had been. Yet at the same time, the ability of the upper end of the social scale to thrive did not miss a beat.

Tackling social inequality is complex and disparities in wealth alone does not account for why some children are able to improve their life chances whilst others do not. For researchers, the worry is that even by the age of three, children from poorer backgrounds are already falling behind. Teachers are aware of a gap between poorer children and those from richer families from the day they arrive at school, in terms of vocabulary and cognitive skills.

One teacher with over 20 years' experience working in primary schools said that during the first week at her Reception class, the new intake of four-year-olds are asked to draw a picture of themselves and write their names. She revealed that from that one picture, she can predict precisely what level a child will achieve at the age of 11.

She is aware that parents would be alarmed to think that any child could be pigeon-holed at such an early age, which is why she remains anonymous, but in her experience, how the child executes that one picture reveals a great deal. It demonstrates a child's ability to hold a pencil, concentrate on the task, and to remember where the features of a face are placed. Those skills rely on attention, memory and symbolic thinking – a capacity that is nurtured by the stimulation a child receives in the early years. This educator, like many others, believes that a child's life chances are fixed even before they take their first steps into the school playground. That is not to say that parents from poorer backgrounds cannot provide a stimulating and responsive environment in the early years. Equally, parents from well-off backgrounds do neglect their children. Interestingly, psychologist Oliver James has written a great deal about the need to provide young children with a stable and responsive environment.

Financially, Oliver James's childhood was privileged but he believes that his mother's mild depression meant that when it came to parenting, 'her mood was one of resignation, with an undertow of anger.' He considers that this led to what he characterises as his 'electrochemical thermostat' being set at 'angry', 'risk-taking' and 'sad' modes, and, as a boy, he admits that he was frequently aggressive. He broke another boy's arm during one confrontation. But facing his late teens, he had the resources to break out of a destructive cycle and decided to study hard and he went on to gain a place at Cambridge.

Depression does affect the ability of a parent to provide a stable emotional environment and a number of studies throughout the UK have shown that rates of depression and anxiety are far higher in deprived areas than in those that are affluent. What triggers depression cannot be credited to a single factor. Likewise, what shapes each of us is an interplay of emotional, interpersonal and social factors both at an individual level but also at a family and social level.

These considerations may sound remote because in the mind of most parents is merely the desire to do all they can to ensure their child's happiness. Providing what is needed and putting your own needs second to that of your child is the ideal attitude, but it is not one that it is possible to live up to at all times. It is a particularly difficult aspiration for those who did not receive good parenting themselves in early life – the blueprint then has to be made from scratch.

Moat's upbringing had been far from ideal but now, as a father, would he repeat the mistakes of his past or would he be able to provide his daughters with better opportunities to thrive than he had received?

By the time that Raoul's third daughter was born, he knew a great deal about how fragile a sense of family could be. He didn't want that for Chanel. He wanted to make things right this time and ensure that his little princess would want for nothing.

He had secured a house in Fenham Hall Drive in Fenham, a three bedroom semi-detached that he was confident would be a suitable family home that he was going to need. His first two daughters from his relationship with Marissa were now living with him, and had been since October 2006. Relations were strained between him and his ex and she could see them on a limited basis only.

It was far from the end of the matter however, and Moat was feeling increasingly hemmed in because of his dealings with social services. As a department, their role is to place the safety and wellbeing of children first, but Moat felt increasingly frustrated and antagonised by their examination of his role as a father.

He was prone to outbursts of anger and staff documented his aggression. The mode of expression that served him well on the street was proving detrimental when it came to dealing with authority. And Moat's response to his run-ins with the police and social services is revealing. He asked for help but he also tried to take control of the forces he believed were deliberately misrepresenting him.

He installed CCTV cameras and began recording his conversations with social and other council workers. He accused them of lying and suggested they were corrupt and seemed increasingly at the end of his tether when it came to accounting for his actions and the allegations made against him.

At one point he said: 'I was up in court on two charges for allegations that social had made, that are proven to be false in court through CCTV, through all the recordings, and I'm still getting crucified for it now.'

The pressure of battling against allegations was building, but by installing CCTV he felt he had wrested back some measure of control, a way of hitting back at agencies that had the potential to break up the new family unit he'd formed. He placed the cameras not just in highly visible spots but under hedges too, as he was determined to monitor every moment that council staff or police entered his property.

Yet Moat also spoke of the need to address his temperament. He is heard saying during one of his meetings with social workers: 'You know, it's easy for me to say I don't do anything wrong but I would like a professional, you know, not a DIY thing you know? A professional thing for someone to come along and say: "Look there's area for improvement here, this is a problem".'

Views as to why Moat reached out this way are divided. Some say that it was a clear cry for help, a recognition that his volatility was a problem that was affecting his ability to parent. Others are not convinced, since those with a Narcissistic Personality Disorder are perfectly capable of saying what needs to be heard if they know that it will further their ends.

There are mixed reports as to what happened after Moat spoke of his acceptance that he might need help. A spokesman for Newcastle City Council said that a psychiatric report had been carried out but that it was part of confidential family court proceedings. He added: 'This report did not recommend any treatment, but examined Mr Moat's aggressive behaviour on the safety and wellbeing of the children…It didn't recommend any treatment because it wasn't about Mr Moat, it was about the safety of the children.'

In the final analysis, custody had been awarded to Moat in 2006 and so there cannot have been sufficiently robust evidence to justify why the children should not be under his guardianship.

The house in Fenham Hall Drive had plenty of toys and the garden at the back would be somewhere where they could play but it was not what Moat wished for his children even if it was adequate for now. In one call to a social worker he says: 'I'll quite enjoy the peace to get away from the police.' He went on: 'This is the kinda place we were talking about. Me and Sam were talking about getting somewhere out in the sticks. I'm the farmer type.' In another conversation he says: 'We are hoping to get a bit of farmland. She wants horses, which will be ideal for the kids. I like the idea of animals, I cannot get used to the city, I cannot get used to it at all.'

It seems strange to think of Moat, a man who'd grown up in the city and made the areas he lived in his own in many respects, talk about it as a place he cannot get used to. Things were changing in his life, he was ageing and the physicality he had long relied on was no longer a point of certainty for him. During one of the taped conversation he says: 'If you use your body like a machine it's going to break – like a machine it'll break down.

'I did martial arts from being young, that was always my thing. When you do something and you excel at it, you want to do it more, but if you do it for too long your body starts to show the wear and tear.

'I just go and lift a few weights now and enjoy it. It keeps us looking good and keeps us fit for the kids.'

His children were always his concern but his ability to provide a stable environment for them was repeatedly under question. There is a sense that Moat kept treading water, but in his fight with various authorities, he was no longer certain how long he could keep his head above water.

It was strange that Moat also taped some of his conversations with his daughters. Was this simply something to remember them by or another demonstration of a need to control his environment? Of course he could simply have forgotten to turn the recording equipment off, but in one exchange he talks to one of the girls about his grandmother, the woman who had been a constant in his early life. He is heard to say: 'You know who you take after? You take after my granny because she was very little.

'She's very special to me. She brought me up. And you've got her tiny little hands and tiny little feet. And you have got what I had as a kid, you have got my little freckles.

'When I was a kid I looked nothing like I do now. I had one of the smallest noses you would ever get on a kid, freckles and ginger hair.'

Indeed, there was very little of the younger Moat in the man who stared back at him when he looked in the mirror. He was now his mid-thirties. He'd lost touch with his brother, no longer wanted to know his mother, and his grandmother had been dead for some time. A lot of his past was little more than memories. He'd come a long way but rather than his achievements making him feel more secure about his surroundings, he felt less so.

Moat was not part of the traditional working class — that class, in that part of the world, had long gone. He was now part of an outsider class, men who did not have a traditional path to work and advancement, men who could not expect their children to go on to excel and achieve, characters who dipped in and out of a grey economy, making cash in hand here and there but who saw threats to their livelihoods from the overbearing role of the authorities on all sides. Their kids could be taken, their cars impounded, their occupations low skilled and low status, their lives existing on the fringes of a society that did not value them.

His voice on the phone is heard to say: 'I'm living my life on the edge, just trying to get by till this next thing and then there's another one and another one. None of this is right, it's not.'

He was a man trying to create a future, one where he could take his children to the country and live in peace, but it was an impossible dream. In truth, he had no faith in the future anymore. He felt assailed on every side, and an idyllic life in Rothbury always seemed beyond his grasp.

CHAPTER FIFTEEN
BETTER OFF DEAD
THURSDAY 8 JULY

Now when I see him I don't recognise him at all.
– from an interview with Josephine Healey

The Raoul Moat story also happens to be one of two sets of brothers. Raoul had a brother Angus, but the policeman he had shot actually had a twin. PC Rathband's sibling Darren stood on the steps of the hospital that was treating his twin brother David and spoke with great composure. He said: 'He's got a long road ahead of him. His family will support him.

'The chief constable of Northumbria Police has assured him that he's got a career within the service that he's served for 11 years and, even now, he wants to still continue to serve the community of Northumbria.

'My brother is an inspiration not only to me. He should be an inspiration to everybody involved in this investigation. He wants to thank Northumbria officers and all the other officers from across the country who've come up here to resolve this incident.'

His only note of anger came when, for a moment, he recalled how his brother had been defenceless when Moat targeted him. He said: 'He was unarmed, parked, doing his job. This coward has not only wrecked his life but the lives of so many people, including his children. He should be ashamed.'

The search for Moat had entered its sixth day. At the same time that Darren Rathband was giving the press an update on his brother's condition, the police had surrounded a remote farmhouse and outbuildings near Rothbury, following up yet another lead; but once again, Moat was nowhere to be found.

Northumbria Police's media centre were under continual pressure to release information to the local and national press as well as to field media enquiries 24 hours a day. There were those who had never worked on an enquiry of this scope before, although it was probable that they would not do so again for many years. At media centres, there is a tension between serving the needs of the enquiry, collating the information that the public need to hear, and maintaining relationships with local press. These different aims need to function well long after the national media has moved on to the next big story.

There are also difficulties for local newspapers following a story that draws national attention. In Newcastle *The Chronicle*, for example, had a difficult line to walk. Its reporters did not have the 'cheque book' leverage of the nationals but it did use its superior local knowledge and contacts to good effect. Reporters were able to provide insight from residents and those caught up in events whilst keeping track with some of the more sensational claims about Moat that would break in the tabloids.

On the whole, relations between each of the 43 police services and the local media are normally cordial. Off the record, officers claim that they have far more confidence that local media will relay details of a case in a responsible way, and this can certainly be in marked contrast to some of the tabloid coverage a big case will attract.

Although the tabloids can sometimes be accused of chasing sensation headlines, sometimes police officers can be frustrated in their attempts to relay key information. One example involved the investigation of the murder of Amelie Delagrange on Twickenham Green in 2004. The Metropolitan police suspected that the killing was linked to that of Marsha McDonnell a year earlier. Both women had suffered severe head injuries after being beaten with a blunt instrument.

The national press immediately coined the term

'Hammer Killer', although the police stressed that the weapon could have been another object entirely – a crowbar for example. The concern was that as the murder weapon had not been found, members of the public might discount other heavy objects because of the fixation on a hammer.

The local press continued to circulate information as requested but the abiding image was that of a 'hammer killer'. In fact, when Levi Bellfield was sentenced to three life sentences in 2008, not only was the weapon he used not conclusively proved to be a hammer, he had attempted to murder another victim, Kate Sheedy, by driving over her in his car. Like many multiple killers, Bellfield's methods could not be summed up in one headline alone.

Northumbria police did issue a statement that morning, again stressing that the police were doing everything possible and striking a note of reassurance for local residents. It read:

Search for Raoul Thomas Moat in Rothbury area continues

The search for Raoul Thomas Moat has continued in the area around Rothbury in Northumberland overnight.

Armed officers and supporting specialist search teams conducted a thorough search throughout the hours of darkness, supported by resources including the dog section. Searches in the area will carry on today as the intensive activity to trace Moat continues.

Temporary Deputy Chief Constable Jim Campbell said: 'I'd like to again thank the residents of Rothbury for their support and patience at what is an unprecedented level of activity for them to see in their rural location.

'The searches in this area have proved a particular challenge due to the open farmland and dense woodland and officers are continuing in their efforts today. I'd like to reassure the public that we are doing everything possible to locate Moat and bring this investigation to a conclusion.

'Although much of the enquiry centres on Rothbury the events in this area are just one part of a complex investigation and activity continues across the force. Our enquiries so far have led to two men being charged in connection with the investigation and they will appear in court this morning.'

Police also renewed their appeal for help from the public to trace Moat.

T/DCC Campbell added: 'We continue to seek help from the public to trace him and if anyone sees him they should call the police straight away. They should also report any suspicious activity to us.'

If this statement was meant to lend an air of measured calm

to the day, it was about to be shattered. The *Sun* ran pictures of a six-year-old Moat and noted that he'd gone from 'cherubic ginger haired boy' to 'psycho commando' but in fact, it wasn't a tabloid but a broadsheet that rocked the course of the operation.

That morning an interview with Josephine Healey appeared in the *Daily Telegraph*. Speaking about her youngest son she said: 'I feel like he hasn't been my son since he was 19 years old. He now has a totally different character, attitude and manner. Now when I see him I don't recognise him at all ... If I was to make an appeal I would say he would be better dead.'

The press conference that had been scheduled for 11am that morning was set back without explanation and seemed on the verge of being cancelled when it was quickly convened two hours late. Temporary Chief Constable Sue Sim told the reporters gathered that information had emerged that suggested that Moat was a threat to the public. This was a significant shift and the media pressed for more details but nothing more was said by way of elaboration.

Detective Chief Superintendent Neil Adamson wanted to focus on information he wanted to highlight. He reiterated that a £10,000 reward was available for information leading to Moat's capture and made an appeal to the 'individual who rang at 10.30pm yesterday regarding a motor vehicle potentially used over the past few days.' Reporters in the room, however, were disinterested in anything at that point other than what had been said by Moat or what information had come in to the police to suggest that the public would now be targets of the killer's rage.

Adamson excersised even greater control with replies such as: 'I have already answered that question'. Then again, in another incident, when one journalist began a question with: 'Without wanting to cause any widespread panic...' only to have Adamson cut in with: 'And it is important you don't.'

What reporters didn't know was that Moat has heard about his mother's interview. In fact he'd heard about a number of stories that had been running in the media and he had become enraged. The police knew this because they had found a Dictaphone at a tent that Moat had being using – there was little doubt that they were meant to discover the tent and the message. The recording was over four hours long and the gunman said he would kill a member of the public every time he read something inaccurate in the press. Bizarrely, he said: 'I am no Derrick Bird. I won't be shooting old ladies in their bobble hats.'

Professor of psychology Craig Jackson believes Moat made this distinction because he wanted to separate himself from Bird and that his ego would not allow himself to be seen as cast in Bird's mould. Jackson says: 'In shooting a police officer, Moat had transformed himself from jealous boyfriend to a 'mission killer', he did not want to be cast as inadequate as Bird had been. By claiming to be 'at war' with the police, he cast himself in his own mind as a heroic figure.'

Psychologists working with the police were alarmed by this development and the decision was taken by Northumbria police to ask the press to agree to a second voluntary black out. After the press conference that had turned decidedly tense, reporters were spoken to off the record and then a letter was sent out to news organisations. The letter contained the following:

'Your reporters wanted to understand the context in which the warning was given. It was therefore decided that we would explain to the press "off the record" the rationale and facts behind our request.

'Putting it bluntly this is a potential life and death situation. The information we have from Mr Moat is that he is upset by some of the press reporting.

'Unfortunately, we do not know exactly what he objects to. The reporting itself may be accurate – we are talking about his perception.

'We have taken advice from a consultant forensic psychologist. It is clear that Mr Moat's rules have changed and that he is getting angrier.

'Mr Moat has said that every time he reads something about himself in the media which he considers to be inaccurate he will kill a member of the public.'

Cooperation was sought and it was given. Not only did the media cease to report on any more 'personal' details, stories were taken down from websites and the tape was not mentioned.

The recording Moat had left was long and often incoherent but it seemed that Moat now saw journalists, too, as possible targets. It was hardly surprising. His paranoia had been fermenting over years and now a new threat had emerged to him in the form of 'inaccurate' coverage and in broadcasting his mother's views that he would be better off dead. All the rage he felt towards her would have been impossible to contain, in his eyes. She had turned her back on him once more and thought him redundant and shameful.

For those advising the force an added concern came when Moat was heard to say that he would call the police before he killed his first victim. To date, Moat had carried out his threats and there was no reason to question that he would back out of this new change to his 'rules of engagement.'

No doubt there was an edge of desperation to this development. Once again, Moat had found that the choices he had made had resulted not in gaining control of a situation, but watching as it further spiralled from his grasp.

He had wanted to teach Sam a lesson, he had intended to show her that she could not walk out on him and take Chanel away too. In a murderous rage, he executed Chris Brown in an attempt to assuage his sense of sexual jealousy and humiliation. Instead of appearing as someone fighting for his rights, he was labelled a monster, a psycho, a cross-dresser, an abuser and a madman.

His attempt to strike back at the authorities he believed were hounding him had led him to raise a gun and shoot a police officer, showing that 'the hunted became the hunter.' But in fact, he shot a defenceless father-of-two in the face as he sat doing his job. David Rathband understood the importance of family, he was a provider and a loving husband and father. He dealt with his injuries with incredible fortitude and has told reporters that he does not feel bitterness towards his attacker. He remains committed to his job and his family, regardless of the extent of his injuries. His brother had been right to call him both an inspiration and the true hero of the piece.

Moat will have felt the full weight of the contrast between the two men he had become and it hit him hard. All his attempts to make his way as a man in the world had failed; he had lost the woman he loved and the children he cherished. And his sense of inadequacy – something that had always haunted him – was inescapable. What was he now? A killer and a monster demonised by news coverage. Now his mother had told a reporter that he was better off dead.

By telling the authorities that he was now willing to kill members of the public, he was demonstrating his need for the police to feel some of the fear that lay within him. He was trying to displace his terrors again, as he had every time he had been violent to those around him. It was his last attempt to lead the police rather than face the stark truth of his situation. He was trapped in Rothbury. The one place that had given him shelter had now become a snare.

He was spotted by a local resident later that day, crouching and moving along the wall next to the village allotments. He entered one of the greenhouses but soon left. No doubt he had been searching for food, but when the allotment owner was eventually allowed back into his greenhouse, he noticed that all that had been taken was the only ripe tomato on offer.

Raoul Moat was hungry and tired. His hyper vigilance could carry him only so far. His enemies had numbers, he did not. They had police and military hardware and expertise, he did not. They had rest periods, warm beds and food, he did not. He could not live like this indefinitely. How did he think this was going to end?

Early that evening, Temporary Chief Constable Sue Sim and her colleague Chief Superintendent Mark Dennett were due to attend a community meeting with residents of Rothbury to answer any concerns they might have. Sue Sim had provided an update earlier that day after the voluntary news blackout that was in place, as there was still a need to provide information to the wider public. She said: 'I want to update you on where we are with this investigation.

'I am aware that this enquiry is now entering its sixth day and I want to make it absolutely clear that we are as committed today as we were at the start.

'From the outset we have stressed Mr Moat's grievances are largely directed towards police.

'Information has now emerged that Mr Moat has made threats towards the wider public.

'I want to stress we have the resources and resilience to deal with this situation and my officers are out in large numbers to provide reassurance and protection.

'It is also important to note that not only are my own officers dedicated to finding Mr Moat and protecting the public, we have also received overwhelming support from colleagues across the country.

'Northumbria Police is leading this investigation. The other forces are providing us with any expertise they have to deal with such situations.

'We are also being advised by the National Search Centre who have particular detailed knowledge about the options available to us.

'The Serious and Organised Crime Agency and the military have also been approached for advice.

'You will be aware that armoured vehicles have been sent from the Police Service of Northern Ireland. These are better equipped to deal with the challenging terrain we are working in and offer improved protection to our unarmed officers, who are still patrolling in Northumberland.

'I've already mentioned how challenging the terrain is. This is a beautiful part of Northumberland but it is extremely difficult to search. The area is full of hills, ravines, caves, dense woodland and deep water. This search will take time and we must protect all those involved.

'Our intention remains to apprehend Raoul Moat safely and bring this to an end.

'I also want to again thank the people of Rothbury for their continued co-operation and support. I visited the town myself yesterday and met many local people. I was delighted to see they were going about their business as usual, supported by my neighbourhood and armed response officers.

'I also spoke to many of my officers in the area. Their determination and focus to help bring this incident to a conclusion remains unwavering.

'Finally I would like to appeal to everyone – the public and the media – for their continued patience and ask that my officers are given the space they need to carry out their duties without being hindered.'

Sue Sim, with her unwieldy title of Temporary Chief Constable, had only been in the role for three months and was in the post whilst Northumbria sought to recruit a new permanent chief constable after the retirement of Mike Craik. She became the focus of comments that often had little to do with her professional role. Comments about her hair, her make-up and even her enunciation was proof that women in the media gaze are judged as much for their appearance as they are for their competence. It is an unfortunate by-product of the intense nature of today's rolling news footage that comments were made as widely online as they were in newspapers. 'Mumsnet' devoted a thread to Ms Sim, anonymous police officers blogged about her appearance too, and it was clear that the operation in Northumberland was fodder for any number of views and topics for debate. The Moat hunt was proving to be an insight into more than modern policing.

The meeting with residents even took on a 'town hall' meeting aspect, more characteristic of those held in the United States. Police forces serve their communities of course, and in recent years forces have worked harder to appear more transparent and responsive to community needs. The meeting that evening at the Jubilee Hall was packed and Sue Sim sought to alleviate any unnecessary concern about Moat's next moves and his threat to the public, saying: 'There has been a change to his circumstances, and I am not saying that he will be walking down the street with a gun, but there has been a change to his circumstances which may bring the wider public into this issue.'

Residents were however advised not to go into the hills or woods as that could potentially put them at risk and, for the police, create one of the worst case scenarios: that Moat might take a local person hostage. The main thrust of concerns from those gathered was for the safety of children and so Sim made it clear that she was willing to act on concerns and said: 'If you are telling us it would make you happier to see police officers at the schools then we will put officers at the schools.' The meeting broke up at around 8pm and, on the whole, residents were satisfied that the police were doing everything possible to catch Moat and to return their town to its normal pace.

There is always a tension between the methodical and patient nature of conducting an enquiry and the heart-racing moment when a breakthrough appears to be at hand. This had happened late on Wednesday night when a caller contacted the police claiming to be Moat. In the first few seconds of the call, it seemed that this was a crucial contact but within minutes it was clear that the call was a hoax. Such irrelevancies are frustrating factors in any high profile investigation.

Detectives on murder enquires have to become accustomed to hoax callers, people who call the team to make false accusations against someone they have a grudge against, or those who call with details they have dreamt up (either because they are mistaken, malicious or unbalanced). They know that each telephone conversation has to be followed up.

Hundreds of calls had been made to Northumbria police by day six and each one locked up man-hours. Even if they were followed up and failed to result in new and valid information being uncovered, there was still a risk that something unforeseen could go amiss. It had happened the evening before when a Rothbury resident, Mr Robert Storer, had called the police because concerns had been raised that someone may have broken into empty property just outside the village. The building belonged to friends of Mr Storer but as the armed response readied itself, one of the police dogs bit Mr Storer in the hand, causing him to need hospital treatment.

Despite the best efforts of the police to maintain a controlled and calm presence, all officers knew that events were by their very nature beyond their control. Anything could happen and after the meeting at the Jubilee Hall had broken up, perhaps it had. Raoul Moat was seen walking down Rothbury High Street.

Only a few hours after Sue Sim had said: 'I am not saying that he will be walking down the street with a gun...' two calls came in to police to say that they suspected that he just had. Perhaps he was not visibly armed but the witnesses were confident that they had just seen Britain's most wanted man strolling through the town.

It seemed an extraordinary stunt if it were true and officers frantically tried to assess whether the sightings were accurate. Police by this point were receiving specialist advice from the army – those trained to track and those with a detailed understanding of how to evade capture. There was a good deal of press speculation that the SAS were involved in the hunt by this stage but that would be impossible to verify. A former SAS soldier, Eddie McGee, had been involved in tracking Barry Prudom during the attempt to apprehend him 28 years earlier and, since that time, the profile of the elite unit had soared.

Two former soldiers from the regiment had both written books about their experiences in the first Gulf war as part of Bravo Two Zero patrol. Since then, both Andy McNab and Chris Ryan have gone on to become household names and have penned a number of bestsellers. A large part of the appeal of their books is the blurring of fiction and what life as an SAS solider is really like and it is interesting that they are both asked to provide views in newspapers whenever issues that brush on survival or the military arise. McNab provided a lot of commentary in the *Sun* and perhaps it was not surprising that Chris Ryan gave his views on Raoul Moat's attempts to evade capture.

Ryan wrote an article for the *Daily Mail* and, although he pointed out that while around Rothbury there were plenty of opportunities to find things to eat and water to drink, it was not the physical demands that would be Moat's greatest difficulty but the battle with isolation. He wrote: 'It is the ultimate test of initiative and the human spirit. Only the most resilient prevail.'

Daylight hours are long and having to stay motionless once a suitable hideout has been found is far more taxing on the body and mind than anyone without experience of such extremes will appreciate. It becomes hard not to listen to your demons. For Moat, the mix of inertia, fear and the gnawing realisation that every decision he had made since leaving prison had been the wrong one, will have been inescapable. All his letters and tapes could not change the fact that he was a killer. Ryan believed that Moat was out of his depth.

If Moat had indeed walked down the High Street late on Thursday evening, perhaps it was a sign that the pressures of existing in isolation were proving too great. Friends would later point to this being a moment where he was effectively hoping to be captured, wishing to bring his attempts to evade police to an end. It would have made an extraordinary sight, as the witnesses that saw him did not report that he was agitated or harried. He was simply walking, almost a parody of the way he had once been able to take his time strolling in the village.

Yet PC Rathband and Samantha Stobbart also both spoke of the strange emotional blankness that they saw in

Moat just before he used his gun, the absence of the man's humanity as he enacted a dark terror. Could Moat have been in such a frame of mind again, taking ownership of the one place Temporary Chief Constable Sue Sim had said he would not appear? Was this supremely provocative?

The hunt had taken on an unreal quality, there were further details yet to emerge that pointed to an odd mix of TV celebrity, media profile and reality. Ray Mears had joined the hunt. Since 1994 this man has been a presenter of television programmes about the wilderness, bushcraft and survival, and perhaps Moat had watched some of his shows. Or maybe decision makers at Northumbria police were Ray Mears fans, because the presenter was approached for advice after Moat's camp had been found. He agreed to help and perhaps both the police and Moat will have appreciated his maxim: 'You don't need equipment, you need knowledge to survive in the wild.'

Mears is undoubtedly an expert but on the section of his website that reads: 'What's Ray up to?' it certainly didn't indicate that he was in the wilds of Northumbria tracking a fugitive. There is without doubt an overlap between 'expert' and potential TV celebrity status today, in part because the needs of 24-hour TV scheduling demands a high output and because 'reality' shows of all hue have become popular.

Ray Mears is hugely popular and has done a great deal to raise interest in the outdoors. There is so great a demand for his hand-made 'Woodlore Knife' that customers are now advised: 'For those customers who have added their names to our Waiting List since 2008, the waiting time is likely to be around 10 years plus.' There is a thirst for authenticity, whether that should be the exploits of Andy McNab or the 'Woodlore Knife' of Ray Mears. And so it was an odd moment to note that the popular TV presenter had been called back to his 'day job' in providing information about tracking, and it can only be imagined what the army specialists, with years of training of their own, thought of the development.

The RAF entered the mix at this stage with news that one of its Tornado jets had been recruited in the search for Moat. It had taken off at dusk that evening as the belief of those tracking him was that this was the time that Moat was most likely to be moving around in his search for food and water. The jet has specialised on-board cameras designed to pick up movement, the same technology that has been used to assist missions in Afghanistan.

This caused some members of the public to question why, along with helicopters, armoured cars, armed response vehicles, two hundred personnel on the ground, trained dogs and assorted 'expert' advice, was it that the combined effort had failed to find one man with a Mohican hairstyle and using camping equipment from B&Q? The operation risked tipping into farce and Moat's continued evasion was gathering an element of support that few had reckoned with. He was developing into an antihero, a Ned Kelly-like figure who appeared to be outwitting the police, their hardware and their multi-faceted expertise.

Kelly was an Australian bushranger who came into conflict with the police and went on the run in 1878. He killed three officers before being captured in a standoff where he appeared wearing home-made metal armour. He was hanged in 1880 but instead of being despised as a criminal, he became a folk hero, still familiar to many 130 years later, because of his defiance in the face of authority. The fact that he left families without husbands and fathers became secondary to the desire for an iconic figure to fill that role of heroic outlaw.

It is interesting to note that notoriety does alter perception. There was a furore in Australia two years ago when the bones of Kelly and other criminals that had been hanged at Melbourne's Pentridge Prison had been discovered. Plans were put forward to commemorate the site and plant a rose garden. Victims of crime groups condemned the move but the comments of Noel McNamara, Crime Victims Support Association chief, revealed the contradiction at the heart of how men like Kelly are viewed.

He said: 'Ned was probably a cop killer and a horse thief, but he is a bit of legendary figure. He should be removed to Glenrowan with the rest of the historical stuff. But the others are just scumbags – the lowest of the low. And there's no way we should be glorifying these people.'

The others will have committed crimes comparable to Kelly's own but Kelly's own 'worth' had been transformed from one of cop-killer to legend and anti-authoritarian hero. The difference between not glorifying 'scumbags' and acknowledging a 'legendary figure' is key. Not all criminals are written off as lowlifes, some ascend to higher place in folklore and are not wholly condemned; some are even celebrated for their exploits.

Moat may well have been aware of this phenomenon, and, by casting himself as 'anti-police' he was tapping into the broader antagonisms of those who feel unfairly treated by authority. Perhaps it was not a conscious step and maybe he was merely at the end of a long struggle against what he saw as all that was wrong in his life, but, by day six, the interest in how he would be apprehended had, for some, become a hope that he'd remain on the run.

For commentators in remote corridors of power or behind the desks of news organisations, such a surge in sympathy for Moat was inexplicable. Just how much of a groundswell of support and just what it signified was yet to be played out. For now, the focus of the police was on the task in hand, the concern for the powers-that-be was only for the situation to be resolved swiftly and with no more loss of life. And for the media, the requirement was to keep filling column inches and airtime.

Raoul Moat had added to the number of papers sold and in some cases, such as local publications, the rise was significant. It would not be spoken of openly but for reporters chasing a big story, this is when the job is at its best: it is when reputations can be made. When the story runs its course there can be an element of disappointment.

It would become apparent that everyone would take something different from the Moat 'story'; it would be a learning curve for policing, it would be by-lines and a job well done for reporters and, for a minority, it would be something to cheer on from the sofa as the 'infotainment' rolled on. Once again, Moat was not in control of how he was seen, how he was viewed, or how he would be judged.

For Moat, attempts to keep being heard and to present himself as a well-meaning and loving man kept coming. Bizarrely, he had managed to get hold of a 'Get Well' card and he sat down and decided to write a message for Samantha. It was mailed to Gateshead Queen Elizabeth's hospital where she was recovering from her ordeal. The card had a picture of a cartoon monkey with a thermometer in its mouth. It read: 'You're in hospital...but luckily the doctors say you'll be normal in no time!' Inside the inscription was: 'Well that'll be a first.' Beneath it, Moat had written, 'No joke intended. Get well soon. Raoul.'

It was an extraordinary gesture. He had shot and killed Chris Brown to punish Samantha. He then shot her in the stomach and it was a very real possibility that she could have died. Now he was sending a Get Well card from his hideout as he evaded capture from the police. How was it possible that he could reconcile his actions with this gesture of concern? In reality, he couldn't – no rational mind could.

Moat still had a need to show Sam that he was there to 'care' for her, it was a role that, along with being a father, he had seen as central to his life over the last six years and he could not relinquish it. Despite the arguments, the times he had hit her and threatened her and made her fearful, he still wanted her to validate him and know that he would not forget her.

Needless to say, the card's arrival was terrifying for Sam. Despite having an armed guard at her door, the communication had unnerved her and made her see Raoul's madness for what it was.

For Professor Craig Jackson, it was yet another insight into how Moat still needed to control Sam and manipulate how he presented himself to the world – as a caring man. Caring men don't kill people with a shotgun; they don't blind and maim others when they feel upset. They may feel anger and rejection, but at their core they understand why restraint is a necessary function of being a good person. Control, in the true sense, means self-control, control of one's ego. It means the ability to understand the views and needs of others and to accept that they will not always chime with your own.

There are masculine traits that perhaps are not lauded enough. Restraint, humility, forbearance and selflessness – they are functions of an inner strength and are not evident in physique and muscularity. They may not be characteristics that will lead to a spread in *Hello!* or have won a candidate selection for *Big Brother*, but they are undoubtedly what allows families and society to function at their best.

'You knew exactly what I was capable of, especially over you, but kept pushing. You killed me and him long before I pulled the trigger.' So read the letter that Sam also saw on the day of the Get Well card's arrival. The police had found it in Moat's tent; it was addressed to Sam and was brought to her in hospital to see if his ex-girlfriend could offer any more insight into the man's frame of mind.

Moat had reduced his actions to a singularity. It was not his fault. None of it was. *'All these years the police have plagued my life, stitching me whenever they can, you've seen it, yet threaten me with your boyfriend to do the same. Last night you made it clear that everything in my life was gone, and you knew what was coming, I warned you, I warned you both.'* Sam had apparently brought this catastrophe on herself. It wasn't down to him.

Again, he expected more of her than he did of himself; when in his eyes, she 'crossed over' to join the ranks of those who had persecuted and let him down, she brought retribution on herself, not him. He was at once, the executioner – the one who controlled who would suffer – but also a puppet, it was *beyond* his control.

'My life was over, so his was too. You on the other hand I don't want to kill. Your shell had less powder, just to give you a surface wound, and through the glass from a distance would ensure that.

'However this has two purposes. The main one being that you will get lots of compensation to bring up our daughter, so in effect I've provided for her beyond the grave…

'The money you will get will take care of you and Chanel so it's not a total loss.'

A surface wound. Apparently to ensure that Sam could not forget him, to mark her as his, so that every other man would see his display on her flesh; a mark of ownership that could not be eradicated as easily as she had eradicated him by deleting his pictures on her Facebook page and changing her status to single. This had been an electronic reminder, in an electronic age, of how casually he could be erased.

This was not the first time that Facebook had become a feature in a murder case, there have been a number of occasions in recent years where it has acted as a flashpoint for domestic violence. In 2008 Wayne Forrester, a 34-year-old lorry driver, was jailed for life after he admitted killing his wife Emma. She had changed her online profile to 'single' four days after he had moved out of their marital home in Croydon, South London.

Forrester told the police: 'Emma and I had just split up.

She forced me out. She then posted messages on an internet website telling everyone she had left me and was looking to meet other men.

'I loved Emma and felt totally devastated and humiliated about what she had done to me.'

Enraged, Forrester drove to the house in the early hours and brutally murdered his ex with a meat cleaver and kitchen knife. This horrific murder would be just one of over 100 murders every year carried out by a former husband or partner.

'Humiliation' in the minds of some men produces catastrophic consequences. Men who fail to confront and control their rage and sense of entitlement and go on to carry out acts of unforgivable violence.

There are also those men who are 'family annihilators', males who kill not only their partners but their children, unbalanced by depression and the belief that if they cannot provide for their family or keep the family unit intact, they would all be better off dead. Each case is complex and there are different roots to the cause of such violent episodes but Professor Neil Websdale, of Northern Arizona University, conducted a study of family annihilators and believes that such killers share a common trait: the feeling that they've fallen short of the societal ideals of manhood.

Many of the men had a string of failed businesses or were struggling financially. These men – Webdale calls them 'civil reputable' killers – see the annihilation as an ill-conceived act of altruism. There was an aspect of that thinking in Moat. By stating that Chanel and Sam would now be in receipt of 'money', Moat was also positioning himself as provider: another key male role. The irony of why Sam would need to make a claim for compensation from the victim support fund seemed lost on him at that point. That 'it's not a total loss' was another attempt to justify the unjustifiable.

But Moat in fact seems closer to the group of men Webdale calls 'livid coercive' killers. This group, Webdale believes, share common characteristics, namely, they feel inadequate as men and frequently they will have suffered childhood abuse. Having felt powerless as children, many try to exert strict control over their households and seek to create an idealised version of family, almost to compensate for that which they never experienced when growing up. Commonly however, men with a 'livid coercive' personality create crises in their relationships with women because of their controlling and abusive behaviour. They are adept at creating excuses for their actions, blaming the activities of others for prompting their outbursts.

Raoul Moat's written attempts to justify and defend what had happened would not have been significant to the police at that stage; the killer had already fleshed out these arguments in the letter he left to Andy MacAllister. What had changed was in the following extract and it was a chilling admission that this was an endgame. Moat had written: 'I'm a dead man walking, but funny enough I feel like a huge weight is off my shoulders…I have a lot of killing to do and they're random targets. This will be the remainder of my days.'

The fugitive knew his remaining days were few and that there was even a measure of relief in that; a certainty and an end to fear when for many, many years of his life he had struggled to find either. But he would not go quietly; it was too late for that. He wanted a final reckoning and he still felt pain, a pain he could not contain. And so once again, the only way he could give it expression was by lashing out. He had a lot of killing to do. A lot more people must suffer as he could not suffer alone, not with the end so close.

CHAPTER SIXTEEN
2009

A police officer's lot is not always a happy one. Try a Friday or a Saturday night out maintaining public order. Being jeered at is nothing, it is the swearing, the spitting and punches thrown as you continue to address the catastrophically drunk as 'sir' and 'madam' which can soon lose its charm.

Transporting the violently inebriated to the police station or escorting them to hospital so that they can get stitched up after an altercation, only to have to restrain them from hitting a triage nurse is at once stressful and repetitive. Not everyone is happy to see a police officer and there are certain sections of particular communities where they are viewed as an enemy as soon as their high visibility vests comes into view. Blame is never far away either – the police are condemned for not doing enough on the one hand, and for being heavy handed on the other.

They see the worst excesses of human behaviour, including cruelty, deceit and degradation. They walk into rooms that are so filthy that they can barely take a breath, only to see a toddler crawl by. If they have to do the 'death knock' and tell a parent that their child has been killed the experience never leaves them. All police officers can do is grow thicker skins, accept that people will lie to them and will hate them, and get through their shifts with the blackest of black humour.

Officers with more experience will teach junior colleagues the ropes. Not the stuff written down, or the endless courses they have to attend or the procedures to adhere to, but the insights that just might save their skin. Such as if you ever have to go into a house to pick up a suspect, it isn't the men you have to worry about but the womenfolk. An irate mother who thinks she's protecting her son will be far more of a handful than a bloke will ever be. And if a house stinks, breathe through your mouth.

Or the tip that you should always leave a man with his pride. It doesn't matter what he's done or what you need to do, if a man feels backed into a corner and humiliated, that's when he'll most likely kick off. Go along with the pretence if you need to, make sure he's got enough room to salvage some face.

Knowing how to handle certain aspects of human nature, making quick assessments and being able to change tack is essential if officers are going to do the job well. In some ways, these are skills that can't be taught. Training is one thing but the best professionals have an instinct for 'the job'. Experience helps but being a police officer relies on innate abilities to read people and a situation and manage its outcome.

Take 'pulling over' a car or van. It might not be the most glamorous and high profile aspect of policing but checking whether vehicles are roadworthy and that drivers are using the roads responsibly will save more lives each year than most other roles of policing combined. But no one likes to be pulled over by the police. Some motorists are contrite and accept that they have been exceeding the speed limit, but these are in a minority. And for the men that are pulled over because there is a problem with their vehicle, being aggrieved is the norm.

When two officers indicated that Raoul Moat had to pull over, they saw straightaway that here was a man with a very short fuse. One wrong word and he could easily escalate his irritation into violence, that much was clear, and the two traffic officers communicated as much to each other with little more than a look. He was big, over six foot tall, very well-built and exuded an attitude that meant that the officers had to present the facts to him in a clear but palatable way, which would be quite a challenge, since they were about to confiscate his van.

The vehicle had been pulled over because it was loaded with scrap metal but was only licensed to carry garden waste. One of the officers got on the radio to create the impression that their supervisor was making the decision, not them. They emphasised that they could understand his point of view and that this wasn't personal.

They had their own pressures, ensuring that if they were to be quizzed by a senior officer, they could demonstrate that they had done what was expected of them. Remaining calm and professional in the face of the motorist's ire is part of the job and both officers sensed that if they lost control of the situation, Moat would be a very difficult man to restrain.

In fact, neither of them fancied the prospect of wrestling him into a patrol car and later one said: 'He was not a happy man. I consider myself fit and I go to the gym but this man was clearly taking steroids and was obviously working extremely hard at the gym. He was huge.' He also mentioned that Moat looked like a man who could rip him in half, yet the officer managed the situation sensitively and there was no altercation.

The officer had years of experience he could rely on and yet there was something about Moat that he could not forget, something about the air of menace he gave off. That officer was PC David Rathband, the man who Moat would take his fury out on a year later.

Moat was furious. Once again, he felt that he had been

targeted and, once again, the authorities were trying to prevent him getting on with his life. He had set himself up as a tree surgeon and landscape gardener five years earlier and had worked hard to build up the business. There was a lot he enjoyed about it – being outside and working suited him and he didn't even mind the paperwork. The seasonal nature of the job brings its pressures though, and it is the nature of any self-employed setup that you can't turn work on and off like a tap. In an ideal world, he would have been maintaining gardens on a retainer, tidying up regular places each month, but those are the contracts that are always harder to come by.

Most of his work had come to him when people had a problem, such as a tree that was so big it was blocking a neighbour's light, or roots that were pushing up paving stones. He employed one or two others when the job demanded it and was happy to help others out when he could, offering to cut one of his elderly neighbour's hedges for her. She appreciated that; she thought that it was rare these days for any of the younger generation to be considerate enough to help out the elderly.

His business was not going to make him a millionaire but it was enough for now, and since Chanel had been born and the three girls were living with him and Sam under one roof, it all should have been okay. But it wasn't. Moat's oldest friend, Tony Laidler, remembers visiting him at home and he noticed that his pal was rubbing his face.

Laidler said: 'We were both getting harassed off the police but it started to really get to him. He always used to rub his face when he got stressed and whenever I went round he was sitting on the sofa rubbing his face.'

Laidler knew that his difficulties were not just based on the stress of finding business. He was upset too that an Environmental Agency officer had been to see him over allegations of fly-tipping. Nothing was proved but in Moat's mind it was yet another example of how he was being hounded.

The business consultant that had helped him set up his business, which was called Mr Trimmit, did not doubt his commitment to hard work – Moat advertised his services as being available seven days a week – but was concerned about the anger that overcame his client when he thought about his run-ins with the authorities. Trimmit said: 'Often his anger would come back to the police, he would say they were always trying to stop him, he would get really upset and say "they are after me".'

For anyone suffering from an underlying paranoid personality disorder, stress and anxiety can heighten the condition and delusions can result. Moat was taping his conversations and had CCTV footage as he tried to get a grip on events that were happening and find 'proof' of the conspiracy against him. At one point when he becomes agitated at the extent to which he might be a target for the police, he is heard on tape questioning if police are making up death threats against his life so that he will be provoked into buying a gun. He said: 'I think it's a deliberate attempt to get me wound up. It's part of the hunting season on Mr Moat by Northumbria Police.'

Whilst to an impartial observer his remarks mark him out as paranoid and delusional, amongst his friends he found a degree of sympathy. For men who are getting by on the margins of society, Moat's outlook was not dismissed. And the reason for that is the uncomfortable fact that to certain sections of society, the outsider class, police are no longer viewed as an institution that is there to protect and serve. They consider the force to exist as a means of social control. The police are seen as enforcers: there to bust you for not having a tax disc, or a TV licence, there to make money for their pension pots from their speed cameras, there when your home is repossessed or your kids are taken away.

Although it is clear to an impartial observer that the ire aimed at the police is misplaced, it is important to acknowledge that it exists if the environment that Moat existed in is to be fully understood. When he raged against the police and other institutions of authority, few around him will have challenged his thinking. His friends saw Moat as a 'good bloke' trying to get by and someone who had always been willing to help them out. They saw his grievances as legitimate.

They talk now about knowing that Moat had personal problems, that things weren't right but there again, having problems was commonplace. In June, he was charged with common assault against a child. In July, events took a turn for the worse. His two daughters from the relationship with Marissa were taken into care. When they were appointed a carer, Moat came to clash frequently with Social Services. It is easy to understand why, in his mind, he was judged an inadequate parent.

On top of the frustrations he faced with Social Services, he was dealing with low-level and ongoing aggravation on the street, his tyres were slashed and window broken. The extent of how much of Moat's life was unravelling wasn't known, just how close to the edge he was went unnoticed. One friend admitted that he'd lost touch with him at one stage because he was struggling with his own problems. It was often the way when relationships broke up, men moved on and attempted to get their lives in some sort of order again. Another friend said: 'You've no idea how bad it can be around here. It's a shit hole. I'm going to leave. There's no point anymore.' The same man had lost touch with his eldest child after an earlier relationship broke down and was trying to use Facebook to make contact. 'There are so many kids with the same name though, I don't know if it will work,' he added. 'I just want them to know that I tried.'

CHAPTER SEVENTEEN
NO WAY OUT
FRIDAY 9 JULY

Sound as a pound. Nowt wrong with him.
– from Paul Gascoigne's Real Radio interview

The arrests kept coming; this time, a man and a woman were arrested in Blyth, a town thirteen miles to the north east of Newcastle.

As part of the 'fast-moving and complex operation', a number of people who had known Moat found that they had questions to answer. It is rare for a murder enquiry, apart from a gangland killing, to involve the arrests of so many people but this had long ago stopped being an ordinary enquiry and now, quite suddenly, it was drawing to an end.

At 10:30am that morning, the police had released images

of Moat's camping equipment and Detective Chief Superintendent Adamson reiterated once more that they believed that Moat was still in Rothbury. But it was two hours later that an update came that showed that the police had at last made some headway. Three mobile phones had been found; one had been handed in by a member of the public and police had located the other two.

The phones were a significant breakthrough as they would allow investigators to piece together more about how events unfolded by checking incoming calls, outgoing calls and contacts made by Moat from before the time of the shootings in Birtley, to the blasting of PC Rathband and the week that Moat had been on the run. They would be vital evidence for any subsequent trial.

The tone of the press statement revealed that the police now sensed that they were closing in on Moat:

Friday 9 July, 2010 – 12:30 Update
Police are making significant progress in the search for Raoul Thomas Moat with a number of key developments over the last 24 hours...

And three phones used by Mr Moat have been recovered.

The first was found in Birtley in the early hours of Saturday morning at the scene of the first two shootings.

A second phone, used to make the two 999 calls to

police before and after the shooting of PC David Rathband has also been recovered – although police are not saying from where or when.

And a third phone used by Mr Moat was recovered yesterday by a member of the public who was out walking in open land in the Rothbury area.... Police know where and when the second and third phones were purchased but are not releasing this information at the present time.

Det Chief Superintendent Neil Adamson said: "There have been some very positive developments over the past 24 hours. I am certain that these phones were all used by Mr Moat. We have recovered valuable information from them and are pursuing numerous leads in connection with this information. This shows the vital role the public are playing in this enquiry and I would urge anyone with information to contact Northumbria Police or Crimestoppers."

Not everything was going the way the press office would have liked to see that Friday however. After the media centre had been part of arrangements to film part of the community work the policing team were carrying out that day, the TV cameras were broadcasting live when Neighbourhood Inspector Sue Peart, sitting next to Temporary Chief Constable Sue Sim, read out a card of support from local children in an attempt to show that the local community did appreciate the efforts the police were making.

Peart said: 'Two little girls came into the police station just last night and they handed me this card. It's addressed to all of the Police Force. I'd like to read what it says: To everyone that's trying to get this nutter off the streets, we would like to say, thank you very much for putting your lives in danger to save ours.'

After hearing Moat described as a 'nutter', Sue Sim was seen to briefly laugh and an apology from the police quickly followed. The term nutter cannot have been helpful as part of the carefully orchestrated communication that had been directed to 'Mr Moat'. Perhaps Sue Sim laughed in recognition of the reality that 24-hour coverage of an event is bound to lead to the occasional verbal gaffe. Sim herself had said earlier in the hunt that 'No stone will be unturned in the search for Mr Moat.'

The metaphor is of course ordinarily used to relay the fact that the search would be comprehensive and, with so many boots on the ground and aircraft with thermal imaging equipment in the air, it seemed incredible that Moat was still evading the police after seven days. It took Search Advisor Inspector Ken Crossley to again underline just what the search teams were up against.

After stating that he found this part of Northumbria 'a fantastic part of the world' and 'beautiful', he then pointed out that the terrain was a problem, with heavy woodland, hills, rivers, caves and dense foliage, and that meant searching each area was going to be a slow process. Added to that they were dealing with an armed man who was desperately trying to avoid capture. As a Search Advisor, Ken Crossley was aware that his responsibility was to consider the safety of the men he was leading. Privately they knew that the area could not be 'contained', it was too great, and everyone involved in the search knew that the threat to their lives was real.

That day, the National Trust property Cragside House and Gardens was closed and cordoned off by the police, and a search of the grounds was carried out. It is an impressive property and grounds but, as the name suggests, it is built on a rocky crag. As the search was underway, perhaps the Search Advisors noted ruefully that that visitors to the grounds are advised: 'Challenging terrain and distances. Stout footwear essential.'

Another potential hiding place was in the storm drains, which run under the main street of the village and out to the riverbank. Work had been carried out on these after the floods of September 2008. The village had been one of the worst affected in the county when the Coquet burst its banks and residents were cut off from the surrounding world. Evacuations were made and temporary accommodation was set up in Jubilee Hall. The metre-wide pipes were installed a year later as a precaution and were also designed to take flood water from the hills that stand behind the village and then out to the River Coquet.

It would be possible to use the drains and even for Moat to have pushed open one of the manhole covers for drains that ran under the High Street and emerged out onto the road. That could explain the sightings that had been made of Moat on Thursday evening. It was a woman who first saw him; he was wearing a baseball cap and she thought that his face looked slimmer than it did in the now-familiar picture that had been distributed by the police. She smiled at him initially, as this was a natural reaction for most Rothbury residents, and she described his expression as sheepish as he looked away. It was only then that she realised that it was Moat and for him to appear to be 'sheepish', after the furore whipped up about Moat being a 'psycho', was something of a surprise. If this was Moat, he was still able to behave in a composed manner – he didn't look like a madman on the prowl.

And yet when, two days earlier, Detective Chief Superintendent Adamson described Moat as, 'a measured individual who appears to carefully plan his actions and is comfortable in an outdoor environment', that now seemed wide of the mark too. It is likely that Adamson was again attempting to create a rapport with Moat by suggesting that they were all impressed by his skills at evasion. If Moat did have a Narcissistic Personality Disorder, this statement will have flattered him and boosted his sense of having superior intelligence and prowess.

Either strolling down the High Street was a sign that he felt invulnerable, or he was indifferent as to whether he would be apprehended or not. A true survivalist would not be spotted and an actual maniac would have killed others, taken hostages, or attempted to kill one of the hundreds of officers scouring the countryside.

In many ways, since his arrival in Rothbury, it had been day after day of inertia. Moat hadn't done anything. He'd broken into houses and taken bread or fallen asleep, he'd taken tomatoes from allotments, and he'd done the bare minimum to feed his body. But he had not brought the 'war' he had spoken of to the forces of law and order.

As the mounting police and army activity swirled around the village of Rothbury, at the centre of it, Moat had slumped into a torpor. His only concrete actions centred around Sam. He sent her a card. He wrote her a letter. He wanted her to listen to him. In his last letter to Sam, he wrote: 'You were everything I ever wanted, and knowing I can never feel the same for another, just makes it all pointless. I've lost everything so this was the inevitable end.'

He had idealised Sam and it was not an image she or any other woman could live up to. When she failed him, he had punished her in the past and his decision to kill his rival was the ultimate sanction. As he ended his letter, he wrote: 'I didn't want any of this but it's done now.'

It was done now. And despite his evasion, he was done

too. He made no serious attempt to leave Rothbury, mostly he waited, unable to focus any more of his depleted energy on escape or commit himself to the 'war' he had promised he would bring.

Channel 4 had spoken to former-SAS soldier Andy McNab and he revealed that search efforts would focus on the attempt to 'channel' Moat to a capture zone. Basically, to avoid an armed confrontation, search teams would be moving through the wooded areas and disturbing the environment so that Moat would move, much as you would attempt to corral an animal.

In fact, that wasn't what would flush Moat out. It was another of McNab's insights that perhaps explains what was about to unfold. He said: 'So many people lose their bottle when being searched for. Movement gives away your location. If you have the bottle, your best tactic is to stay still. If you can keep still, calm and make yourself feel safe, the chances are those searching for you will simply walk right past you.'

Movement would give Moat away. His threats against the wider public had come to nought. It was light, not yet 7pm and Moat wandered back towards the river, close to some stepping stones that mark one of the favoured walks that attract holiday-makers to the village.

There was some suggestion that he had already been seen near the bowling green and tennis courts and that, as police officers came into view, he headed towards the river and a chase began. If Moat intended to keep on the run, this was a poor choice. He had cut himself off with the river behind him and a road in front. There was a sudden frenzy of activity as news that Moat had been spotted broke over the radios. Vehicles and officers began to gather in numbers. Two police cars collided but the area where a man could be seen lying on the ground with a gun to his neck was quickly contained.

The press release when it came was one of the briefest of the operation but the impact it had was immediate. It read:

Friday 9 July, 2010 – 19:00 Update
A man who fits the description of Raoul Thomas Moat has been located in the riverbank area in the vicinity of Rothbury. Police are currently negotiating.

The operation now swung into another phase. Local residents were advised to stay indoors and a charade began between the press and the police as the latter attempted to keep journalists and cameramen at a safe distance and the media did all they could to get as close to the river as possible.

After a week on the run, seeing Moat now crouched at the side of the river hardly seemed real. Traffic had been stopped entering the village from the east, there was an exclusion zone in place around the site, vehicles and armed officers in body protectors were in place, two ambulances were on standby and the figure in front of them had sat down.

Dressed in a baseball cap and wearing a dark top, Moat had not been rushed because it was clear that he was holding a shotgun to his head. In the moments after he had been pushed back to the river, residents say that they heard a lot of shouting. But now there was silence and a negotiator who had been brought to the scene knew that the first task was to keep Moat calm.

In the mind of every officer there it was painfully clear that there could be any one of three outcomes. Either Moat would commit suicide, he would come out shooting or he would give himself up. He wasn't going to be able to get away.

Back in the city that Raoul Moat had fled from, Samantha's grandmother, Agnes Hornby, said: 'He's not a scaredy-cat type of person. I thought he would come out shooting, so they would shoot him.' Even having never met Moat, that will have been a prime concern.

A phenomenon now recognised in the United States is 'suicide by cop'. In the US, it refers to an individual who wishes to die and uses the police to effect that goal. It is a contentious subject, as police respond to situations without prior information about the state of mind of the individual provoking an armed response.

In one instance in Philadelphia, police responded to a

burglary-in-progress call at a school. The suspect was spotted by the police and he opened fire, shooting twice. He was chased through the building and cornered by a police dog-handler but his gun was trained on the police. Officers opened fire and killed the man. Later, it was established that not only was the gun a starter pistol incapable of firing live rounds, but that the man who made the call about the break-in at the school was the man they shot. This was a suicide arranged by a subject who had previously been hospitalised after a less successful attempt to kill himself.

Although police officers in Philadelphia knew nothing about that man's background and state of mind, the officers on the ground at the river Coquet knew a great deal more about Raoul Moat. If he had wanted to kill himself, why had he not already done so? If he had wanted to start picking off officers or members of the public, why had he not made any attempt to do so whilst hiding out in Rothbury? Why if he wanted to give up, had he not handed himself in? As Moat sat on the grass, the likelihood that this was building up to be 'suicide by cop' could not be discounted.

The negotiator at the scene was hoping for a very different outcome. Only 20 feet away from his subject, it was relatively easy to call out to Moat and also to hear his responses. The hunted man was lying down, the gun still visible and pointed to his head. It was a stalemate: if police attempted to rush him he would either attempt to shoot one of the officers or kill himself. But of course it was not a stalemate. Moat no longer had any cards to play except to threaten his own life. As Channel 4's Alex Thompson blogged live from the scene: 'If this is indeed Raoul Moat, and it is indeed a standoff, the police now have it on their terms in a reasonably secured area from which "civilians" have been long since cleared.'

Blogs, tweets, rolling news cameras – the standoff was delivered into homes, mobile phones and computers just like every other big news event. Just like the blogs, tweets and rolling news that had played out in parallel on news services updating fans on the progress, or lack of it, of the England team in the World Cup. England had crashed out 12 days earlier after losing to Germany and the final between Spain and the Netherlands was two days off. That night, Moat became the number one trending topic on Twitter. It was possible to follow the build-up to the final and monitor events in Rothbury simultaneously that Friday night, and many people did.

That was irrelevant to the officers on the ground, the senior officers coordinating events at the river, the snipers in position watching Moat's every move and the negotiator trying to resume a dialogue with Moat as daylight faded. There were two groups of armed police positioned on each side of Moat. Their role was to monitor him and should the need arise, shoot him, should he open fire on them or their colleagues. They were also in place to rush Moat if the opportunity arose, or to simply arrest and contain him if he was to throw down his weapon.

These teams are taught and trained to demonstrate two key abilities. First, infinite patience. It takes as long as it takes and remaining 'in position' and immobile for hours at a stretch is part of the job. Yet, at the same time, the other ability the officers have to demonstrate is moving quickly and effectively at a split second's notice. The police called this stage of the operation 'live and fluid'. Despite the training, the drills and the simulated exercises, this had an entirely different quality. The threat was real, immediate and unpredictable and yet, crouched in position, with cramp setting in and the temperature dropping, the need for total focus was absolute.

By 9.20pm, the police made it clear that they wanted the media to move back. Not by the few hundred yards that they had requested earlier. The majority ignored this embargo, skirting back to the area where Moat was being penned and even knocking on doors and holing up in homes until the police had passed by and they could move freely again. This time the police wanted the media to withdraw to 10 miles away.

That was simply never going to happen. They stressed that media presence was interfering with their ability to negotiate but most journalists weren't buying that. There were those amongst them who'd reported from war-torn assignments and so one man with a shotgun to his head wasn't going to deter them. Journalists could be seen climbing over garden walls and heading back to 'the story'. Most got back to within range of the police vehicles and voices, although they did not have a direct view of Moat.

The negotiators, a team of three, were right to question whether the media were complicating an already very tense situation. If Moat knew he was being watched — and there is evidence to suggest that he had been following the coverage his shootings and his week on the run had generated — then perhaps he would find it impossible to simply put down the gun. How would that look? The big man with all the threats and bravado, just giving up. The world's cameras watching as he would be pounced on, cuffed and led away. After coming this far, how could he end this without humiliating himself?

Moat was talking, that was a positive sign. There were times when he was agitated, when his voice would rise to a shout, but the negotiators managed to calm him. They stressed that he would not be hurt, that he could end this positively and by using his name 'Raoul', they thought there was a good chance that he could be talked around. He was tiring, that was evident. He rubbed his face and it was quite early on in the standoff that he had told them that he had nothing to live for. He then said: 'I haven't got a dad.'

Everyone gathered at the riverside will have known

about his mother's comments that he was better off dead. It was a sign of how isolated Moat felt, which, in turn, was a danger point. He felt alone and he could not imagine a future – a frame of mind most likely to provoke an act of self-inflicted violence or a last burst of aggression. His body language tilted from resignation to agitation. It was clear that this desperate character could not acknowledge his situation or the idea of surrender.

He then said: 'Nobody cares about me.' It was a maudlin remark but also the voice of a child. He was a killer, someone who had maimed his ex out of jealousy and a man who had coldly shot a police officer in the face and hoped that he'd killed him. His actions were brutal and unforgivable. It was hard to reconcile this man with the defeated and pitiable creature at the riverside.

The negotiators focused on distracting Moat and talked of a future, much as the consulting psychologists had advised the police throughout the week. Talk of the future prompted Erwin James, a man who served a life sentence for murder, to question that. He wrote: 'Political considerations would probably have ensured that he was handed a "whole life" tariff. At the very least he would have got a minimum of 35 years, making him 72 before he could apply for parole.' He saw Moat's future as a 'celebrity con', leading to long periods of isolation in special security units and even when inside, he'd be subject to tabloid stories sold by other inmates. He concluded: 'He may indeed have had a future, but not one that anyone would have wished for.'

With his gun held to his neck, Moat would have turned these thoughts over and over in his mind. The negotiators have a range of tactics and hearing a voice other than theirs, a trusted voice, can make a difference. One of Moat's oldest friends, Tony Laidler, was allowed to enter the cordon. He hoped to speak to Moat and talk him out of his despair. He also tried to convince the police that Moat's gun was empty but the police could not take that risk.

Laidler could hear his friend and he could tell that he was distressed but, ultimately, he was not allowed to talk to Moat. He could only talk to a psychologist who in turn would relay his comment to one of the negotiators. As they could not guarantee what Moat would do, the police would not risk a civilian's life and so Laidler could go no further. It was frustrating for Laidler and by this point, when darkness fell and arc lamps were brought in to illuminate the scene, Angus Moat was seeking to talk to his brother too.

Angus had to watch as events unfolded on the television screen. He had contacted the police but he was not taken to Rothbury. He claims that the police told him that although he had not fallen out with Raoul, his presence might unlock childhood memories that would create a potentially more volatile situation. Angus said: 'I'm absolutely convinced that if they'd let me through there, I could have talked him down…I was frantic, I couldn't do anything.' It was also alleged Raoul's uncle, Charlie Alexander, wanted to speak to his nephew too but his request wasn't acted on. The whole incident will be investigated by the IPCC.

It is true that if a subject is under extreme stress, a family member can trigger negative memories and so the introduction of another 'voice' in negotiations has to be managed with care. What the police did not need and what no one expected was that on Newcastle based *Real Radio*, the standoff was about to become a discussion point for ex-Newcastle and England footballer Paul Gascoigne. He wanted to talk about Moat and he wanted to help. The conversation went as follows:

Host: Hello Paul
PG: Hello!
Host: Good evening you are live on Real Radio. I just wonder. Tell us about Raoul Moat. The Raoul Moat that you know.
PG: Raoul Moat, er Raoul I knew him years ago he used to be a bouncer in Newcastle, I knew him a lot of years since I was a young kid, when I play for Newcastle. He was like a gentleman, someone must have wound him up or done sommat, right. And all of a sudden I just listened to the radio right, I mean on TV news. Obviously he's killed someone and he's shot two. Right?
Host. Well

PG: Doesn't matter. He's killed someone. Which is not nice, really. Obviously he must have been on drugs, errrm, and he's shot two people right. Now I've heard on the news that obviously the drugs must have worn off. Now he's willing to give in. Right

Host: I think we have to point out that…

PG: No, please, get a hold of me, no, hear me out, he's a lovely bloke I know that so at the end of the day I think he's frightened in case, errm, he's put his gun down, I know for a fact he will put his gun down but I think he's scared in case the police shoot him and kill him. The drugs have worn off all he wants to do is surrender. And at the end of the day when you shoot someone, I think, and er, shoot, kill someone and shoot two others. you may get what, twelve days, twelve years, twelve…

Host: Paul, Paul, Paul, well we don't know about that exactly. But just tell us, what would you say…

PG: Twelve years, could be about six and you're out. He's a good lad.

Host: If he could hear a message from you Gazza, what would you say to him tonight?

PG: Well I think the police get hold, Listen, I drove from Newcastle in a taxi to Rothbury, cost a lot of money. I brought a dressing gown for him, I brought a big jacket, I brought some chicken, some bread, I know you're going to love this one, I brought him a can of lager, I brought him a fishing rod cause I heard he's by the river. And I brought a fishing rod too, we'll fish together, I'll have a chat with him…just talk and, cause I think I'm the only man…I can help him through this cause I've…

Host: So Gazza, are you going to go to the police and say, let me, let me, let me help you here? I know Raoul Moat. I can help you negotiate. I can help you sort the situation out.

PG: I've just spoke to the police.

Host 2: What did they say Gazza?

PG: That he, well er, er, well…Terry was next to us taking photos and the copper went, police and I said listen, I know the guy, he's a nice guy, I said err, I want to go through, where you have everything all cordoned off, I want to get through there but the police wouldn't let us so that was a waste of time saying, oh, I knew him because they were being frightened he might shoot me, you know? But I told them…he will not shoot me.

Host: Well, it's a dangerous situation though, Gazza, isn't it?

PG: Hey I'm not scared I've just been in a core crash I've just hit the wall at 90 miles per hour. I survived that I'm sure I can survive a bullet. Knowing my luck he'd probably miss.

Host: So what you're saying is that you want to go in there, you want to help negotiate.

PG: …(illegible).. the police know, I want to go in there, I've got a jacket, I've got a dressing gown, I've got some chicken, I've got some bread, I've got a can of lager, I've got a fishing rod, erm, I've got my fishing rod, I'm willing to sit down, to shout, "Moaty, it's Gazza", all I want to shout is "Moaty it's Gazza, where are you" and I guarantee he will shout his name out, "I'm here" and me and him could sit and chat, have a little bit of fishing and all I'll tell him, Moaty. Listen.

Host: And you think you could sort it out?

Host 2: So if you like a man to man chat with him, two pals on a riverbank?

PG: Yeah, yeah, two friends on a riverbank from Newcastle and all those years we'll say is "Why don't you just, you know, put the gun down, throw it in the river and say look Moaty, the worst is the worst you might get a twelve year stretch, the police aren't going to kill you, because I know he's willing to give in now. Whatever he was on has worn off, I mean the police are not going to kill you, he might do a twelve year stretch, obviously for killing someone, which is not very nice obviously he did it cause he was high on drugs probably right.

Host: Paul, have you been in touch with him recently?
PG: For good behaviour he'd get out after six years.
Host: Paul, have you been in touch with him recently?
PG: Have I been in touch with him recently? No, cause I've been in hospital.
Host: When did you last talk to him?
PG: Well, er, I see him, I spoke to him about a year and a half ago when he was in Newcastle.
Host: And when you spoke to him then how was he?
PG: How was he? Sound as a bell. Nowt wrong with him.
Host: Gazza thank you very much for being with us tonight.
PG: He's a bouncer, he's a good lad, he's a hard guy…he's a gentleman but it's not nice when your ex-girlfriend, well his girlfriend ran off with another guy.
Host: Gazza thank you for being with us, we wish you well in your efforts to bring this situation to a peaceful resolution.
PG: Do me a favour, do wish Moaty well, he'll be alright.
Host: I think you've done that already.
PG: I'll look for him…I've come from Newcastle all the way to Rothbury…am gonna stay in bed and breakfast to see if I can find him, I tell you what

he's the only one, I think I can talk to him, and I aint scared.

Host: Paul Gascoigne many thanks for joining us on Real Radio tonight we appreciate it.

PG: Thank you very much, do us a favour?

Host: Go on.

PG: Send a cheque through the post…ha ha ha only joking.

Host: Gazza thank you.

It was a bizarre intervention from the ex-footballer and although the radio interview went out locally, it was soon picked up nationally and added to an already sensational story. Gazza knew Rothbury, he'd been fishing there several times just as Moat had, and it was in Rothbury that Gazza was reported drinking in a local pub during one of his failed attempts to quit the bottle.

The footballer, who was capped fifty-seven times for England, has featured in the press as much for his behaviour off the pitch as on it. He has had a long-standing problem with addiction, has had health problems and has struggled with depression. He admitted in his autobiography that he head-butted his wife Sheryl and smashed her head into the floor and that it was the worst thing he ever did in his life. He talked about his panic attacks, his fear about the facing the future, the sense that he has of himself as a 'jinx' on those around him.

Gazza also knows how he's viewed by the outside world; despite the residual affection people have for him and his days as a footballer when he displayed incredible talent, he believes people don't understand him. In 2004 he said: 'As I get older now I try to cope with things better and talk about them. People don't see this side of Paul Gascoigne. They just think he's a fucking idiot, but inside I have deep feelings.' He thought he understood Moat and in many ways he probably did.

Born in 1967, Gazza was a similar age to Moat and in some ways, it was Gazza's most memorable TV moment that came to shift the boundaries of how we view emotional outpourings. In 1990, Gazza received a yellow card after a foul on Thomas Berthold during England's semi-final against West Germany in the World Cup. If England had gone on to win, Gazza knew that he would not be able to take part as that was his second yellow card and he would have been suspended. Gazza's tears become the defining image of the World Cup in the UK and it ameliorated the fact that he had committed a foul.

After all, by fouling Berthold, Gazza had brought the yellow card on himself. He was so emotional that he also could not take his penalty kick in the shoot-out that followed the 1-1 draw. Once more, England exited the World Cup – as they would again twenty years later – yet, because of Gazza's display of raw emotional disappointment, his transgression was overlooked and he was embraced by the nation. The cycle of emotional outpouring and public sympathy continued through the 1990s; emotion become not only permissible but in some ways expected by those in public life.

Tears shed, trauma shared and tragic events recounted from bulimia to breakdowns are all now the norm on 'reality' TV shows, from contestants on *X Factor* to *Big Brother* to *I'm A Celebrity Get Me Out Of Here*. Whilst there is no doubt that society was ready to move from a classically English 'stiff upper lip' that in many way represented repression, social commentators began to note a new trend emerging – 'recreational grief'.

The height of the huge outpouring of emotion came with the death of Diana, Princess of Wales. Patrick West went on to describe the floral tributes and teddy bears that appeared not just for the Princess but for any high profile tragedy or death as 'conspicuous compassion' and said: 'We live in a post-emotional age, one characterised by crocodile tears and manufactured emotion.'

In truth, Gazza didn't really know the gunman – a friend of Moat has said the footballer would exchange no more than a few words as Moat let him into nightclubs – but that reality wasn't what led Gazza to Rothbury. He felt he knew him. He recognised and responded to the man's despair.

More pertinently for Moat, how we feel is now all too often allowed to dominate what we think and how we behave. Whilst self-expression and being in touch with emotions is a good thing it is naïve to expect that exposure to emotion will solve deeper problems. In fact, Moat found a deeper frustration when he expressed his needs and found that they were not met.

Prioritising hurt and emotion allows self-pity to push aside harder questions of culpability, responsibility and the need for change. Moat had run the full course of his pain and his humiliation and he had exhausted his every emotion during his letter writing and tape recordings. They would stand as a testimony to his frustrations and spent hurt.

Now he had nothing left, just the hours of darkness ahead as he was picked out by arc lights. But perhaps there was something else. Perhaps there was the full realisation that what had brought him to the riverbank with a gun to his neck wasn't the police, wasn't Sam, wasn't the difficulties of his past. He had brought the end, the end he never wanted.

CHAPTER EIGHTEEN
2010

Things had not been good for a while. Moat would get angry with Sam, he'd punch doors, smash ornaments and Sam said that he'd slap her 'every other day' if she upset him.

She would sometimes move out and go and live with her grandmother but Moat would talk her round, apologise and say that things would change. Sam said: 'He would always win me round again by saying he was sorry and how he'd never do it again. He was manipulating me, I can see that now.'

The last straw for Sam came when Moat threw a stool at her and it caught the child. She decided that her daughter could not grow up in that environment and so packed her bags, waited for Moat to go to work the next day and then left. Despite Moat's hope that his house in Fenham would be the answer, it had only served to bear witness to its disintegration. Moat was in trouble now, over a separate issue of domestic assault against a young child. He had been accused of using force but he would not accept it.

In one of the meetings that he taped, he spoke about his inability to keep things on an even keel. He said: 'I'm quite emotionally unstable you know, I get myself over-the-top happy sometimes you know.

'And I have my bad days you know, erm, I've done it all my life that when things [are] going on that you don't like you block things out.

'The more you block things out the more numb you become in the heart you know, you get to a point where happiness to you is just like, you know, neither here nor there.'

Neither here nor there, Moat was in limbo. Sam had told him that it was over but he could not accept that, could not move on; in his mind it was not over. His business was struggling, he had more than one vehicle taken from him, and with the arrest for assault, he doubted that he'd be able to regain custody of the children.

Moat felt he could no longer overcome his problems and yet he had not done anything wrong. He talked to a friend and said: 'Honestly I'm not joking. I've done nothing for five years, nothing not a thing since I packed the doors in, you know, no fights, no straighteners, not even just daft bits and bobs. Kept myself clean as a whistle.

'But, er, but I opened the tree surgery company I was getting the police like taking photographs of my truck and then sending the environment agency round to see if I was fly-tipping man.

'I mean I've got all my bookwork going back ages you know but they left but they're just constantly pulling us, constantly, constantly pulling us.'

Moat was given a court date but he was adamant that he would not plead guilty. It was a risk as if he did, he stood a better chance of receiving a community sentence, not a custodial one. He refused, as an admission would mean that he would be unlikely to have custody of the girls and would have to be supervised if he did have access to them. He decided to fight the charge. He lost.

Despite his size, he spoke to close friends and said that he was nervous about how he'd cope inside. It wasn't that he couldn't handle himself if anyone tried to attack him, it was another fear – of being confined. He lodged an appeal and in the meantime was taken to Durham Prison. Friends tried to reassure him that he'd be fine, that it was a sentence that would last weeks not months, and that he'd be able to pick up the pieces once he got out.

But he no longer believed it and, what was more, once

he heard that the house had gone and that Sam was gone, his thoughts darkened. He knew he would crack, he feared going on a rampage of destruction and even spoke with the prison chaplain. He was still locked up when Derrick Bird carried out his slaughter and Moat saw this as a sign. Not a sign to act the same way, but instead, a warning not to, and he feared being called a monster as Bird had been.

Outwardly in prison, he did cope. He was not taking steroids anymore but did go to the gym, the other inmates saw much they could identify with in Moat. He did fall apart once Sam told him she had met someone else and when he came out, one friend, Anthony Wright, saw something in Moat he had not seen before. They met on the Friday before the killing began and Wright said that Moat spoke about his childhood. Wright said: '…he told me on Friday that being banged up for 23 hours a day had brought back the bad memories of his childhood. We were sitting in the car and he seemed distant.

'His eyes were glazed and he took three or four seconds to respond to anything. It was like things weren't registering properly. I tried to get his spirits up by cracking a few jokes but it was like he wasn't really there.'

In many ways, he wasn't. When Moat wrote on his Facebook page that 'I'm not 21 and I can't rebuild my life' he was facing up to his sense that he did not have the resources to pick himself up again. Wright knew that Moat had done all he could to try and turn his fortunes around before. He said: 'Raoul is no angel. He's been a bit of a bad lad in the past but over the last few years he's made a hell of an effort and slogged his guts out to go straight and turn his life around.

'He came off the steroids, set up his gardening business from scratch and grafted seven days a week to make it work. There are lots of other jobs someone like Raoul could be doing where he could earn a lot more than £50 a day, but he wanted to be legit, above board and settle down.'

Legit, above board; it had not amounted to anything. His former business consultant remembers watching him lift huge tree trunks but his strength would not be enough. He felt that he could not break free and now he had nothing left. Yet it is the line he wrote before his belief that he would not be able to rebuild his life that revealed so much. He wrote: '…to top it all off my lass of six years has gone off with the copper that sent me down.'

Chris Brown, of course, had not sent him down, he wasn't even a policeman, but in Moat's mind, the truth and his imaginings were indistinguishable. All his points of failure, all his rage, was coalescing to one point.

He picked up a shotgun and he made his plans, He shaved his hair, shopped for supplies, packed his gear. He would take the fight to Sam, to Chris Brown, to Northumbria police, to the world.

But Raoul Moat already knew that the battle had been lost.

CHAPTER NINETEEN
AFTERMATH
SATURDAY 10 JULY

You can't outrun a bullet
– from Raoul Moat's letter to Samantha

There had been some encouraging signs as far as the negotiators were concerned; Moat was compliant and had asked for food.

Earlier, he had asked to be allowed to sit up and he got to his knees and rocked from side to side to try and relieve the cramps in his muscles. He'd asked to be allowed to stand up and permission had been granted although officers noted that he did not let go of the gun or even lower it from his neck.

A pack of sandwiches was brought to him along with a bottle of water by two officers moving in behind shields.

He told the negotiator that they must be sealed as he feared that the police would try and drug him. He ate the food and this was encouraging, as a man thinking about ending his life would not ordinarily be thinking about what to eat. But, to counter that, each time Moat was asked to consider giving himself up he would say: 'I don't want to spend the rest of my life in a cell.'

And that was the stark reality. Police could assure him that he would not be hurt, they could talk about a 'future', they could send in food and water but they could not promise anything like freedom.

By 10.30pm, Moat's tone became despairing and he began to repeat that there was no point in going on. The hope for the police had been that they would be able to carry out a 'forensic arrest', namely that they would capture him, splay him out and bag his hands and arms to protect any forensic evidence. A case to show that he was the man responsible for three shootings still had to be built. But the hope of an arrest began to drain away.

It was possible that he was wearing body armour and XREP Tasers might be the best way to penetrate his clothing should he train his gun on the police. They would not open fire on Moat unless he aimed at them directly.

The hours were slowly mounting, teams on the ground were relieved by colleagues but of course there was no relief for Moat. The arrival of arc lights that had been moved into position had coincided with Moat's deterioration. Perhaps the prospect of a long night ahead was too much. Moat would shout out, he had periods when he was incoherent and angry, but his anger was going nowhere.

He shouted out his fear that officers were moving behind him, through the river, that he could not see because of the glare of the lights. The negotiator insisted there was nothing behind him and truthfully, that would have been too high a risk, as any snatch group from behind would have been in danger of gunfire from their colleagues at the front, had shots been fired. But it was clear that despite six hours of talk, Moat did not trust the police.

It was dark, it was after midnight, the negotiators had been brought in and the siege had gone on for hours. Moat was cornered. Snatch squads had edged closer to him in the darkness; it was extremely tense and the end was imminent.

It was over. Moat had fired. There could have been as many as three shots, police officers fired two Tasers. They rushed over to their man, the gun was secured, and paramedics moved in to examine the extent of his injuries. There was a single shotgun wound to the head but officers said that Moat was still breathing. A frantic effort began to give medical assistance to the casualty and he was rushed to hospital. He was confirmed dead at 2:12am, just under an hour after the shot had been heard.

Most members of the public woke up on Saturday

morning to see or hear the main news item: Moat was dead.

Privately, some admitted to a moment of disappointment, because the story that had dominated the news cycle and the blogosphere for a week was over. Barbara Ellen wrote in the *Observer* about the worrying truth that the majority of us had followed the story as a spectator sport. She wrote: 'What was I waiting for – a bit of drama in my feeble little life? When I did turn the TV off, it wasn't because I felt sickened by all the violence and the pointlessness, it was because nothing much was happening. Nothing kicked off until the early hours, which just wasn't convenient TV scheduling for me.'

Raoul Moat had an audience. His audience felt a little let down at the end of it all although would be too polite to say in company and, besides, a new cycle would start up soon enough. It is the nature of the 24-hours rolling news beast, it has to be fed just as it has to be consumed.

But the story was far from over and the aftermath revealed as much about the world Moat never really found his place in, as his week on the run had. He was embraced in cyber-space, one Facebook page 'RIP Raoul Moat you Legend' attracted well over 30,000 followers, but also garnered widespread condemnation and the demand that the page be taken down. The Prime Minister David Cameron condemned it and also frowned on any sympathy for the 'callous murderer'. The lone parent who set the page up, 21-year-old Siobhan O'Dowd from Burnley, soon found herself caught up in tabloid fury.

She refused to take the page down and Facebook resisted pressure too. O'Dowd claimed the right of anyone to have an opinion and, in truth, about half of those who did join the page were condemning Moat and his supporters. But O'Dowd expressed the views of those who did want to hail Moat by saying: 'He kept from eyes of police for a week, that were funny. He were right underneath their nose, right underneath them, and they still couldn't find him.

'I think he's a legend for keeping them on their toes for a week, it's funny how he hid [from them]'

The reaction from the wider public was one of disbelief but also dismissal that this was no more than 'angry white working class' and 'ignorant' opinion. The distance between some of the voices in cyberspace and the sensibilities of those writing opinion pieces in newspapers seemed insurmountable. Moat received a groundswell of sympathy from those who also complained of being 'harassed by the police', for 'not getting help when he needed it' and his ex was the subject of vitriol for 'betraying' Moat. There were ugly exchanges on both sides but, of course, hidden by cyber anonymity it was easy to make the boldest and most shocking of statements.

The *Daily Mail* condemned the sympathy for Moat as 'a disturbing sickness at the heart of our society' but is that what the few thousand messages of support do indicate? The majority of those who claimed to sympathise with Moat also said that what he did was 'wrong'. In whipping outrage about a 'bitter, deluded underclass', the tabloids perhaps missed a broader concern for those at the bottom of the social ladder. Moat 'stuck it to the state apparatus' that appeared to care little about their lot. The one overriding sense was that Moat made the police, with all their hardware, quasi-military get-up, helicopters and jets, look daft. It was one bloke jogging around in a storm drain. People found it funny that the all-powerful state looked inadequate.

There was bellowing about how the same people that condemned the fact that Moat did not get 'help' – from the state-run mental health services – could also lash out at the overbearing influence of the authorities in their lives, but people on the whole have no difficulty in holding two apparently contradictory points of view when they sit behind a keyboard and post how they 'feel'. The news channels constantly ask people to text in their thoughts, no one expects a particularly thorough analysis, just as residents on the streets of Rothbury were continually flagged down by journalists asking how they felt because they needed to fill airtime.

Moat, unwittingly, had become a symbol for something

far bigger than he was. Symbolically, in his own mind, when he shaved his hair, shopped in B&Q, and got hold of a firearm, he was 'standing up', he was refusing to accept his lot. He wanted to exert his control but from the moment he raised his gun and shot Chris Brown, that illusion was shattered.

He re-cast himself as a 'mission killer', out to avenge his ruined life by blaming and then hunting the police. He had transformed himself before, from slight red-haired child, to powerful man and so imagined that by targeting police officers, people would understand.

They didn't. They couldn't. David Rathband was blinded by a man who was blinded by his own sense of outrage. But in targeting the officer who sat alone and unarmed, he attacked not 'state apparatus' but a father of two, a good man and a good husband: all the things Moat hoped to be.

He left his children without a father, just as he had been fatherless. He left Chris Brown, a man who was also a father, dead and his family and friends distraught and grieving. He left his own family, his brother Angus and his Uncle Charlie, with a legacy of grief too. Angus said: 'I had to watch my brother die on national TV.'

We all watched and Moat knew that we watched and it made him unhappier still. And the end, he left an audience. An audience that did not care, that could not care, except for their own concerns.

RAOUL MOAT

At Moat's funeral, coverage would be dominated by the appearance not of family or friends but of Theresa Bystram. She had journeyed from Weybridge, Surrey, with three of her teenage sons, although she did not know Moat. So why was she there? She said: 'I just think he is a hero and I wanted to pay my respects. He kept them coppers on the run all that time.'

For some, Moat had already been cemented into a list of antiheroes. For those who knew him, it seemed wrong. A neighbour of Moat's who attended the funeral said: 'He was no hero. He was messed up. He had problems.'

The funeral had been witnessed by almost as many journalists as it had been by mourners. And yet no matter what the depth of scrutiny to come, the truth behind Raoul Moat's dark decline into despair and violence slips away, not able to compete with what he now represents.

It will be impossible in the final analysis to know what drove Moat. Things were wrong in his life, perhaps they always had been wrong and he stood little chance of making them right. Perhaps his life is not dissimilar to that led by many others like him. But Moat had a choice, in the early hours of a Saturday morning, and he made the wrong one. He gave in to what was darkest in him when he chose to kill and maim.

It was bleak in almost every respect and yet one other voice spoke of what good she thought had emerged from such a catastrophic event, and it was the woman at the centre of the storm: Samantha Stobbart. She sent a card to PC David Rathband, a man still living with pain, living with the knowledge that he has a long road to walk before he can accommodate his disability, a man who has spoken not of regret for himself but regret that he will not see his daughter walk up the aisle on the day of her wedding, or his son wear his cap and gown at his graduation.

Samantha called him a hero and said: 'Witnessing your strength has been a source of great inspiration for me.'

That should be the final act of witness for this terrible and bloody event. Rathband's resolve not to surrender to bitterness is humbling and is evidence of the strength, the true strength, that a man is capable of.